Teaching Shakespeare:
A Trilogy

by Keir Cutler, PhD

Three hit monologues:

Teaching Shakespeare
Teaching Detroit
Teaching As You Like It

ISBN: 978-0-9919280-7-1   (book)
ISBN: 978-0-9919280-8-8 (ebook)

Rights for performance can be arranged by contacting Keir Cutler through his website at www.keircutler.com

IN MEMORY

To my mother, May Cutler,
who was my biggest fan and most valued critic
through the creation and staging of all these works.

I miss you.

TABLE OF CONTENTS

Keir in *Teaching Shakespeare* (1999).

AUTHOR'S NOTE

Teaching Shakespeare: A Trilogy tells the story of Dr. Keir's descent from tenure-track college Shakespeare professor (*Teaching Shakespeare*), down to community college, adult education lecturer (*Teaching Detroit*), and finally to high school substitute teacher (*Teaching As You Like It*). Each monologue is anywhere from a year to a few years apart in time. The age of Dr. Keir is flexible; he can be performed by a young man in his twenties to an older man of almost any age. I was 43 years old when *Teaching Shakespeare* debuted in 1999, and I'm still performing it now at 61.

All three monologues use direct address, pretend the theatre audience is a classroom of students and use a simple desk and chair as a set. The monologues can be performed individually, or together, or even pairing any two of them. I have always performed them individually, but I'd love to see them all performed in one production, possibly by three different actors playing Dr. Keir at different stages of his life.

Performing these three shows has given me enormous pleasure. I've presented them across Canada and in many American cities. Along the way I've also made many good friends, none better than TJ Dawe, who has made a cameo appearance at the end of *Teaching Detroit* on a number of occasions, and was the dramaturge and director of *Teaching As You Like It*. I want to thank him for his wonderful introduction to this book.

Keir Cutler, PhD, May, 2017.

INTRODUCTION
by TJ Dawe

I met Keir at the 1999 Montreal Fringe Festival. I was volunteering as a venue captain, as well as doing one of my monologues in a late night slot at the festival. I saw his new show, *Teaching Shakespeare*, and loved it. Saw it the next year when he remounted it with twenty minutes of new material, bringing it up to fifty minutes. He saw my shows. We hung out. We liked each other's work and company. This led to me doing a cameo in *Teaching Detroit*, and directing and dramaturging *Teaching As You Like It*. And numerous other shows of Keir's that followed.

Keir Cutler's *Teaching Shakespeare* shows are very much a product of the Fringe Festival circuit. Like many successful Fringe shows, the premise of *Teaching Shakespeare*, a dogmatic, deluded professor attempts to teach a class and fails, doesn't have "sure-fire hit" written all over it. If Keir had gone the traditional route, submitting the script to artistic directors, play contests, playwriting development programs and juried festivals, he might not have found someone who wanted to produce it. He may have been steered toward creating a play that has more conventional trappings. He may have listened to those voices. That would have been a shame. *Teaching Shakespeare* and its sequels follow their own paths, and work brilliantly.

Traditional theatres are battleships. Lots of resources needed to keep them going. Plenty of personnel. Strict division of duties. Rigidly hierarchical. Slow to change directions. Fringe shows are speedboats, zodiacs, skiffs, jet-skis, dinghies, miniature pirate ships. There's only room for a tiny crew. They can be operated solo, and often are. One person alone on a boat has to know how to navigate, sail, cook, bail and communicate.

In traditional theatre, the director's job ends on opening night. Actors are hired for a single run of a show. The playwright is there for the development, and the production in their home city, and might be brought in for an out of town opening, if the presenting company has money (very few of them do). On the Fringe Festival circuit, one or two people do pretty much everything: writing, directing, performing, designing, marketing. And they're there for every performance. Learning from every audience. Making discoveries that sometimes take fifty performances to reveal themselves. Tweaking their script and performance as they tour. A show improves in increments large and small.

I believe the best way to learn any form of art is by osmosis. Training is good, but get in the field. If you want to create theatre, see as many plays as you can. Get involved with as many plays as you can. This second part is tricky. Actually, the first one's tricky, too. Theatre is expensive. Except at Fringe Festivals, where it's exceptionally cheap. But the second part, most actors, writers, directors and designers are at the mercy of the Big Machine, which decides that this person will work and all of these others won't. What do you do if you're one of those others, but you have a soul full of creative energy that burns to be expressed? Fringe Festivals let you do that. You can take an idea, get it up on stage, and discover whether it's seaworthy or not, for the lowest production cost you're going to find anywhere.

Performers touring the Fringe circuit see many, many plays. Performers always comp each other in. It's not unusual to see ten or more shows at a single festival. If you want to, you can see five in a single day. You can't help but be influenced by every one of them. The bad ones often teach you more than the good ones, whether you quantify what you're learning or not.

Fringe shows make their box office, and nothing more. Some don't break even, with all the expenses involved in touring. You'd think this would steer creators to stick as closely as possible to what sells, but that isn't the case. Fringe audiences are surprisingly open to new stuff as long as they get it. Play with me, they say. Take me somewhere I've never been. Show me something I've never seen. Don't give me the same old same old. So most Fringe shows ride the line straddling the experimental and the accessible.

Touring Fringe artists interact with other artists. We see each other's work. We talk. We jam at the bar or at the beer tent or on the sidewalk.

We create bits together for late night cabarets. This can lead to deeper collaboration.

People have been telling me for decades that theatre is dead. Subscriptions to the big regional theatres are down. The aging subscribers are dying and not being replaced. But Fringe Festivals are thriving. It isn't big business. No one's getting rich. Fringes aren't crawling with agents and producers looking for the next big thing. No one's getting cherry-picked into the worlds of TV and movies. But the number of people who apply to participate in Fringes grows every year. Audiences are growing, too. Not astronomical numbers, mind you. It's still underground stuff, in the grand scheme of things. And it's vivid, and alive. It's the rats and roaches in the hidden areas of the big ships. The rats have fashioned boats of their own, and set sail.

Theatre is evolving. Some of those big battleships are working hard to patch their leaks. Some are succeeding. Others have sunk. And all of these little speedboats zip around, finding places to go as the landscape changes. Artists are learning their craft on their feet, in front of one audience of strangers after another. Absorbing. Adapting. Fuelled with ideas the Big Machine doesn't have time for. Following artistic impulses that don't have to be sifted through the filter of whether they'll appeal to a conservative subscriber base that wants a sure thing.

As of this writing, Keir has been writing and presenting his stuff at Fringe Festivals for eighteen years. *Teaching Shakespeare* has been alive that long, and it's healthy. Still hitting the road. Still making people laugh. Engaging people in dark rooms. Prompting Keir to keep exploring his ideas, and keep bringing them into the world. To keep living the life of a working theatre artist. Inspiring others to do so as well. Thank you, Keir. And thank you, Fringe circuit.

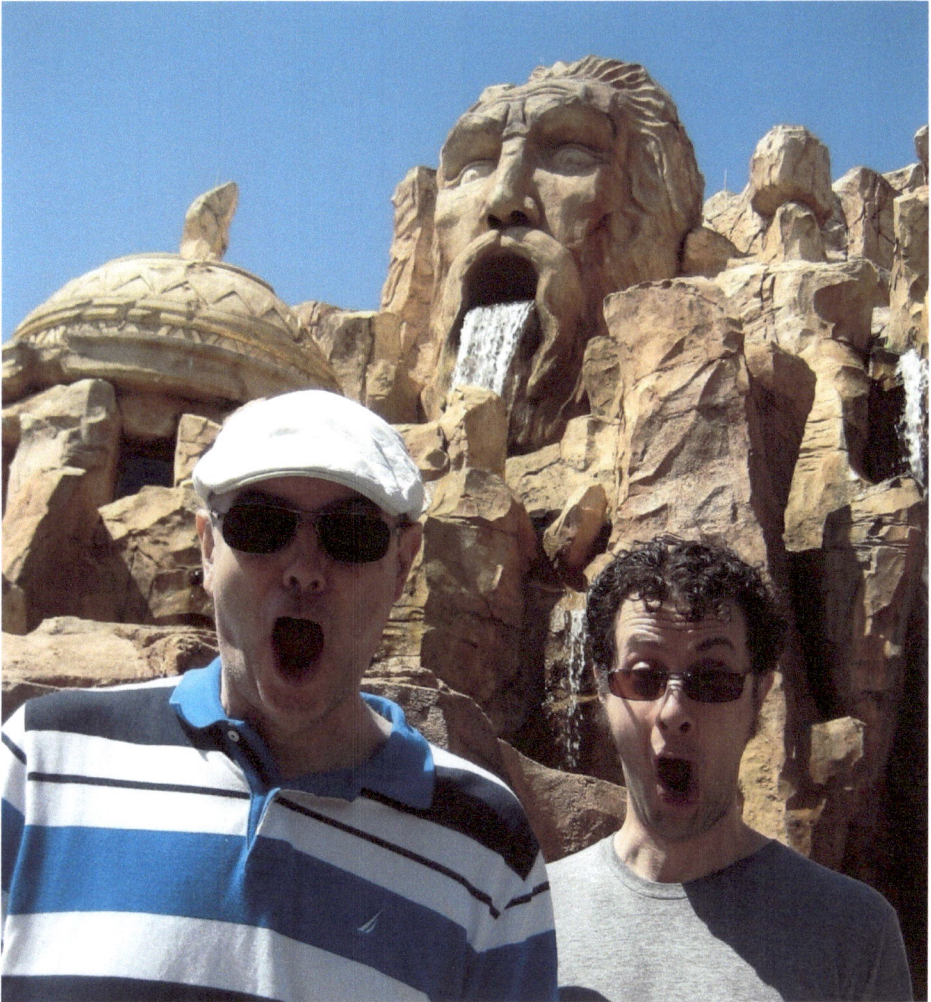

Keir and TJ Dawe in front of Mythos in Orlando, Florida, USA (2014).

ABOUT TEACHING SHAKESPEARE

Teaching Shakespeare, the first monologue in *Teaching Shakespeare: A Trilogy*, debuted at the 1999 Montreal Fringe Festival. As of 2017, the piece has had over 200 performances across North America. It has won several awards, including the "Overall Excellence Award in Solo Performance" at the 2000 New York Fringe Festival, and was filmed and aired on Bravo!/Canada in 2005 as part of "The Singular Series."

Reviews:

"I remember *Teaching Shakespeare* as one of the most enjoyable Fringe productions of the last decade. Actor/academic Keir Cutler gave us Dr. Keir, a self-styled Shakespeare expert giving a university class. It was the class from hell. Keir pulled off the amazing feat of feeding you some fascinating minutiae about Shakespeare while leaving you laughing at the awesome ineptitude of the teacher." Colin MacLean, *Edmonton Sun*

"a richly realized study in disintegration, one man's life slowly coming apart at the seams. . . . A real theatrical gift." Janice Kennedy, *Ottawa Citizen*

" . . . extremely silly and funny . . . . There's nothing wrong with having fun in the theatre, especially when Shakespeare is the subject. . . . I'd give it an 'A.'" Michael Lazan, *Backstage* (New York)

" . . . a very funny, often cutting and totally engaging work . . . formidably delightful." Doug DeVita, *Off-Off Broadway Review* (New York)

" . . . hilarious example of how not to conduct a class in the study of 'The Bard.'" Kieran Grant, *Toronto Sun*

"Original, funny and intelligent." Joanne Huffa, *EYE Weekly* (Toronto)

"Keir Cutler's *Teaching Shakespeare* is the perfect primer for a visit to the Stratford Festival. Intelligent writing, . . . a wicked satire." Pat Donnelly, *The Gazette* (Montreal)

"Blisteringly funny stuff and sometimes ambitiously and beautifully lyrical. It's a first rate text. Go." Gaetan Charlebois, *Hour* (Montreal)

"*Teaching Shakespeare* is playing to sold out houses for a good reason. It's a very funny, witty, well-acted show. I loved it. . . . It's a brilliant way to spend an hour. Go early, tickets are selling out quickly." Sam Mooney, *Mooney on Theatre*

"Keir Cutler's delightful *Teaching Shakespeare*, the most fun I've had at the theatre in years!" Kelly Bedard, myentertainmentworld-theatre.blogspot.com

"In Cutler's laugh-a-minute classroom parody, he is 'Teaching Shakespeare.' . . . Even while being pompous, he seems pathetic—a difficult feat and one that generates laugh after laugh. . . . gloriously funny . . . Shakespeare haters will get the joke. And Shakespeare lovers—if they have a sense of humor—will be rolling in the aisles. Matthew J. Palm, *Orlando Sentinel*

"Supremely witty!" Liz Nicholls, *Edmonton Journal*

"Absolutely hilarious!" Adrian Chamberlain, *Victoria Times Colonist*

Keir in *Teaching Shakespeare* (2004).

TEACHING SHAKESPEARE

(A college classroom. Desk and chair. A briefcase and water bottle are on the desk. Lights up on DR. KEIR with a text of Shakespeare.)

DR. KEIR

Please open your texts to today's scene.
(*opens his text*)
A very interesting scene.
(*studies the scene a few moments*)
Again you have two people who have things that need talking about and yet they are not talking about them. So the scene has an intense emotional heat, but with a tentative shyness. Now her state of personal chaos is a little more heightened than his. However, watch, as we journey through the scene, how aware he is of the precariousness of the circumstances. The whole thing is a setup, because he believes it has to be a setup. It's the difference between ACTING! And real acting.
(*moves around the stage studying his text*)
Lucid prose. That is somehow elegant in its simplicity. By the return to verse. But not complete return. There it is, prose, which is? Can anyone tell me?
(*if someone in the audience replies, he will engage, otherwise he gives the answer*)
The language of everyday speech. Alternating with verse, which is?
(*again, he will momentarily wait for an answer*)
Structured poetry. What can Shakespeare be up to? Hmm?
(*he points to his text twice to show verse, then prose*)
Verse. Prose.
(*turns the page, then points again twice*)
Prose. Verse. But verse where the end of a line is no longer an absolute destination. The phrase carves up the line, runs over the ends of the pages.
(*his hand runs off the page and he moves several feet to one side*)
It comes to a stop where it pleases. And, once again, we see, as character is flawed, so is the poetic meter. Then when the news comes that was hoped for, indeed even believed true . . . magnificent writing!

The metaphorical suggestion that the natural universe is itself aroused and participating in the event. Preparing the audience, the community, indeed all of us for a sort of theatrical miracle.

(throws back his head and laughs, but quickly stops and looks down at the audience, his students)

It's the kind of great rough magic Shakespeare does. We can hear the images. It's almost as if these characters were masked.

(turns the page)

But they are masked! Powerful stuff! Shakespeare is bringing the play back up into the warm light of comedy. And suddenly the world is changed. Supplying us with something not unlike the feeling of the darkness of night being replaced by the gentle light of day.

(goes to back of stage to indicate past, then moves forward)

The idea of the past and the present moving towards the future. We can feel the play moving forward, but moving forward in circles.

(makes circles with one arm)

Here we are mourning a death, while we're about to celebrate a new life. The image is of . . . someone tell me what is the image of this scene. The image is of . . . the unidentifiable. And this goes back to the whole idea of active healing. Which we see throughout the plays of Shakespeare! . . . Though not necessarily this one . . . I find something very moving in the understatement. Look how much room Shakespeare gives us. It's a single heartbeat.

(beats chest once, then slowly extends arm)

And we can take forever with this moment . . . I think it's time we investigate what isn't being said. And indeed sort of give words to whatever that moment was that must have taken place, perhaps offstage. If it happened at all. But we mustn't push it too far because the words do not exist. As always with Shakespeare, things are not what they seem, nor are they otherwise . . . All right, can we focus our attention sufficiently to grasp Shakespeare's inexhaustible catalogue of resources? Can we evolve from being mere students into critics, Shakespearean critics? Yes, I see we can.

(sits on the front of the desk, and puts down the text)

Now while the duty of a critic is to criticize, we as Shakespearean critics have a slightly different task, to defend everything believed to be written by Shakespeare. Assume the author is infallible and has composed a flawless play in which all the various parts cohere into a perfect artistic whole. Defend every part of the play at all costs. If something can't be defended on the page, state that it works in production. If it fails in production, blame the production. Remember the cardinal rule with Shakespeare's writings: Whatever we don't like, we don't understand . . . The quality of his writing operates on such a sophisticated level of genius that there are few actors that can rise beyond a level of simply embarrassing themselves in performance. They imitate humanity so abominably that the theatre has become a place to confuse and repel the seeker of Shakespeare. The poetic brilliance, built on syllabic intensity, structured on the cellular selectivity and omission of the very vowels and consonants that compose Shakespeare's plays is far beyond the sluggish intelligence of actors. And thanks to these thespians, the greatest playwright of all time is held responsible for boring more people than any other human being in history! Is there some way to drive into their minds that the purpose of playing "is to hold as 'twere the mirror up to nature"? . . . "O there be players that I have seen in a play that should be whipped!" Even if you could cast a theatrical genius to play your lead, you'd still need a minor army of genii

> (*he pronounces it, "gene-E-I"*)

to play all the other roles. Every production of Shakespeare is a misrepresentation of the play. It is quite simply impossible to adequately produce a play of Shakespeare's, and that's what makes his plays so riveting! Yet alas, Shakespeare is performed more frequently than any other playwright. So, what do I suggest? Don't attend performances of Shakespeare!

> (*stands*)

But if you must, bring your text, a pocket flashlight and read!

> (*pauses*)

I'm sorry, I have to stop.

> (*stares at the students a moment*)

Students, I have a matter to discuss. It's a personal matter, but it concerns everyone in here. Recently I had the rather unpleasant opportunity of reading your student evaluations of my teaching. Oh, don't think we don't read them.

> (*indicates his briefcase*)

I have them here. Your unsigned evaluations. Shall we take a look?

> (*removes folder from briefcase*)

I have been unjustly accused!
(*reads an evaluation*)
Of "idolizing Shakespeare."
(*reads another*)
"Racing off on tangents."
(*reads others*)
"Springing senseless pop quizzes." Of "conducting the class in a incoherent, unplanned manner." Accused of "being a fraud as a professor by electing to perform for the class rather than teach!" Who wrote this one? "Set him before me, let me see his face." Her face? No, these are anonymous knives, aren't they?
(*closes the folder*)
And finally, and most damningly, universally accused "of never completing the assigned scene during class"! Well! Might I inform you that this year I am up for tenure, and that these slanderous "evaluations" may be—"never completing the assigned scene during class"? Yes . . . well . . . as Shakespeare would say, "A friendly eye could never see such faults."
(*comes forward and kneels*)
Some of you say I place Shakespeare on some literary pedestal far above all critical assessment. I've been chastised for, in a word, "Bardolatry." The worship of the transcendent genius of Shakespeare to which all other men must kneel and strive to comprehend. You see me akin to the writer Herman Melville, who said, "If another Messiah ever comes he will be in Shakespeare's person." Well, I am not unaware of Shakespeare's failings.
(*stands*)
His minor inconsistencies, loose ends. Awkward and undramatic exposition. His inclusion of irrelevant characters. His turning inactivity into action. His sloppy, impossible, even ridiculous plots. His plagiarism.
(*drops folder on desk*)
Sexism. Anti-Semitism. Cannibalism. His inaccurate, blatant errors of chronology and geography, his anachronisms, his blending of comedy and tragedy, his seemingly arbitrary shifting between verse and prose, his coarse jokes and lowbrow puns, his allowing the good to end unhappily, his use of supernatural events to fulfill his tales, his wish to please and rarely to instruct. His only real interests—indiscriminate sex,

shocking violence and crude humor catering to the basest tastes of his vulgar audience, all for immediate effect while he willfully defies logic, believability, morality, the unity of time, place and action. And his shipwrecks not occurring within a hundred miles of a sea!

(*pauses*)

Well, these issues must be ignored. Anyone who repeats them merely resents Shakespeare's greatness. Wants to diminish, to demean, to degrade, to cast down his writings. Well, I will not let this happen! Listen, students, Shakespeare is creating out of words flawed human beings. Unique personalities calling out to our common humanity. They give and receive speech. Whole life, gripping, tearing, developing itself. An extraordinarily dense and alive poetic structure in a universe not at all like ours! What is this universe where our scene exists? Hmm? What is it?

(*pauses, then sits on chair behind table*)

What is Shakespeare's universe? . . . We sit here today in a largely godless place. Faced with the rather unfortunate understanding that we are hurtling through space alone, unwatched, unexplained. Left to wander and weep in cosmological emptiness, while our fellow beings misconstrue us in their evaluations.

(*pauses*)

Thanks to you, I may soon be denied tenure. Denial of tenure is not necessarily a traumatic experience. It is a simple fact of university life. Not the end of the world. Life indeed goes on. It goes on with no career, with financial ruin, with mental health and marital problems, with a foreboding sense of alienation that threatens to—but none of this is of your concern. Why? Because my universe is not the universe of today's scene. No. Imagine instead, there is a God, who has created a connected series of spheres as a universe. A hierarchy where the smallest insect to the highest angel, every being, every thing, all ranked as either inferior to or superior to all other beings and things.

(*stands and reaches above his head*)

First the greatest sphere, *Primum Mobile*, the first mover. Circling all and giving the heavens their motion. Below this greatest of spheres, the stars, all equidistant from the earth like "a most excellent canopy." Then the known planets, each with its own sphere, Saturn, Jupiter, Mars, Venus, Mercury, the sun, the moon and at the center of the universe, the Earth. And at the center of the Earth is man, and at the very center of man, of knowledge, of philosophy, of poetry, of theatre, of all that is known and all that is beginning to be known, is William Shakespeare! All the world is indeed a stage playing to a perfectly balanced harmonious cosmos.

> "but when the planets
> In evil mixture to disorder wander,
> What plagues and what portents! what mutiny!
> What raging of the sea! shaking of earth!
> Commotion in the winds! frights, changes, horrors,
> Divert and crack, rend and deracinate
> The unity and married calm of states."

Shakespeare tells us. By taking just a degree away. "Deracination," to deracinate, to pull up by the roots! Any departure anywhere in the great chain of being and the universe is in mutiny! Shakespeare's analogies, comparisons, relationships, are not poetic metaphors, they are parallel realities. The disruptive force of life contends with the balance of divine pattern, and departure from pattern is character. Fascinating! Think about that. Departure from pattern is character. Get this down. Vowels, consonants, syllables, feet, meter, phrases, lines, sentences, speeches, scenes, acts, plays, characters, persons, family, status, state, stage, audience, actor, theatre, reality, world, COSMOS! Each entity compelling the other to action, all rivals for attention and through it all, even in its departures and deviations, a pulsating iambic verse.

    (*opens and closes hand repeatedly*)

Authority and rebellion, meter and prose, order and chaos, the heartbeat of cosmos. The heartbeat of life. The heartbeat.

    (*opens and closes hand again, and makes throbbing sound of a*
    heartbeat five times)

Iambic pentameter! Ten beats divided into five poetic feet, each foot normally being an iamb, or an unstressed, then stressed, syllable. The basic building block of Shakespearean verse! Like so—

    (*opens and closes hand on each "dee-Dum"*)

dee-Dum, dee-Dum, dee-Dum, dee-Dum, dee-DUM! Has Shakespeare found a way to connect patterned verse with speech-like language?

    (*pauses, looks at students*)

I hear your thoughts. "Verse does not belong in the modern theatre, it is too artificial, too strange, simply too distracting to mirror common speech!" Well.

(*recites next three lines heavily stressing the beat*)

"if YOU have TEARS prePARE to SHED them NOW."
"but SOFT, what LIGHT through YONder WINdow BREAKS."
"a HORSE! a HORSE! my KINGdom FOR a HORSE!"

(*starts "dee-Dum" loud with energy but soon tires and slows*)
dee-Dum, dee-Dum, dee-Dum, dee-Dum, dee-Dum! Dull, stale, tedious? Perhaps.

(*walks very close to students, opens and closes hand, finishing unexpectedly on the syllable "ques"*)
"To be or not to be that is the ques—!"
(*stares at his closed hand, then slowly opens it*)
"...tion."
(*shows his hand to the students*)

Ah what do we have here? Eleven beats. An unstressed syllable extending a line of verse. The feminine ending or the hypercatalectic line. Now why? Why? Why would Shakespeare do this? There are supposed to be ten beats. Here Shakespeare puts eleven, and in his most famous line!

(*pause*)

Because Shakespeare is not writing cheap, monotonous doggerel. He's not a slave to iambic pentameter. Shakespeare's verse is resistant to static rhythm! "To be or not to be that is the question." To leave us hanging, brilliant! An extra syllable in a line is to crowd the air with meanings only half-spoken, partly concealed. As character is flawed so is the meter.

(*opens and closes hand, finishing with an open hand*)
dee-Dum, dee-Dum, dee-Dum, dee-Dum, dee-DUM! Dee. That's William Shakespeare.

(*goes upstage and leans on side of desk*)

Can anyone tell me a single piece of factual information about the person William Shakespeare that you are completely certain of?

(if someone in the audience responds, Dr. Keir will ad-lib a comment, otherwise he continues)

I didn't think so. Is there anyone here who thinks William Shakespeare did not write his works? . . . There'd better not be! This might be a good time to remind you what the great French writer Alexandre Dumas said. Dumas wrote *The Count of Monte Cristo* and *The Three Musketeers*, and Dumas said, "Only God created more than Shakespeare." I can only add, we don't know if there is a God or not. . . . Though I'm forced to admit there is almost nothing known about the person, William Shakespeare. We think he was born in Stratford-upon-Avon, married and had children there. Went to London, where he commenced as an actor. Wrote poems and plays. Retired to Stratford, made his will, died and was buried. dee-Dum, dee-Dum, dee-Dum, dee-Dum, dee-DUM! But perhaps there is a little more. Over about twenty-five years, from 1588 to 1613, Shakespeare created in the appallingly reeking, overcrowded, plague-infested city of London, England. His theatre was a thrust stage in a circular arena, a cross between a castle courtyard and a bear-baiting pit. Bear-baiting was the most popular amusement of the day. A bear or a bull was chained to a stake and four or five hungry dogs were set upon the animal. Most of the dogs would be killed or maimed. Producing, according to a chronicler at the time, "a most delightful spectacle." Theatre plays had to compete with this spectacle. Hence Shakespeare's pornography of violence, *Titus Andronicus*! Condemned by the poet T. S. Eliot as perhaps "the stupidest and most uninspired play ever written." But remember, whatever we don't like, we don't understand. *Titus Andronicus* features gratuitous violence, rape, mutilation, self-maiming, bloody murders, severed hands and tongues, and a climactic banquet in which the Queen is served her two murdered sons in a mincemeat pie. *Titus Andronicus* was in Shakespeare's day, one of his most popular and best loved plays. Ahh. But I have not forgotten today's scene.

(picks up his text)

I will cover today's scene! I will complete today's scene!!!!! Let's read a few passages out loud to soak up the atmosphere, revel in the language, and let Shakespeare's great waves of passion and hilarity break over us as he enters our bloodstreams! But first, can everyone here identify the three basic metrical variations off of the iambic? A brief refresher.

(acts out the three variations with the opening and closing of his hand)

Trochee, a metrical foot characterized by a stressed, then unstressed, syllable. The opposite of the basic iamb. "dee-Dum" becomes "Dum-dee." Used by Shakespeare to suggest?

(looks at students for an answer, then gives it)

The supernatural. "DOU-ble, DOU-ble, TOIL and TROU-ble." Spondee, a metrical foot characterized by two consecutively stressed syllables. "dee-Dum" becomes "Dum-Dum." From Shakespeare, "If music be the food of love, PLAY ON." "Play on" is a spondee. A monosyllabic spondee. Pyrrhic, both syllables of the foot reduced in stress. Not "dee-Dum" but the swift-moving "dee-dee."

(suddenly a flash of anger)

Whoa! Whoa! Whoa! Before any of my evaluators here rises to suggest that Shakespeare was in fact not writing iambic pentameter, but some other form with loose combinations of rhythmical phrases characteristic of the insipid hip-hop rap, let me remind you that this misguided view reduces Shakespeare to an abstract exercise of rhythm without meter and posits the outrageous assertion that my identified iambic patterns, altered by spondees, trochees and pyrrhics, are in fact illusions. NO!

(calms himself, then continues)

All right. Where was I? Don't let me get off the road, because it was a good road . . . oh yes. Pyrrhics! Let's look at an option. Hamlet confronts his father's ghost.

(looks above the audience, apparently seeing a ghost)

"My father. Methinks I see my father."

(looks back down at the audience and explains)

The "her" in "father" and the "me" in "methinks" are reduced in stress. The pyrrhic foot! What can be happening within the absence of syllabic stress? Is there a speechless gasp?

(again looks above the audience, apparently seeing a ghost)

"My father.

(gasps)

Methinks I see my father."

(looks back down at the audience and explains)

Or, or, or does Hamlet's father's ghost breathe within the pyrrhic foot?

(again he looks above the audience)

"My father.

(breathes in very slowly and loudly)
Methinks I see my father."
(looks back down at the audience)
Let's dissect Shakespeare's line. An iamb, followed by a pyrrhic, followed by three consecutive trochees.
"my FA-ther me THINKS i SEE my FA-ther."
(makes hand gestures for the following)
Dee-DUM, dee-dee, DUM-dee, DUM-dee, DUM-dee! YES? Am I good making sense? Yes. Now. Oh, oh, oh! We need to discuss Shakespeare's use of strategic stage absences. Tragic heroes—Hamlet, Othello, Lear—all disappear for extended periods of time late in their plays, and create a significant theatrical effect by their absence. First a demonstration—
(exits and returns after a few seconds)
Good. Now let's examine what just happened.
(gets the chair, brings it in front of table and straddles it)
What was your first question as you saw me leaving the class? Your very first question. Shout it out.
(waits for a response and does not continue until someone says, "Where did he go?")
Yes! Where did he go? Exactly. And your second question, not your final question.
(waits for a response, looking for someone to say, "What's he doing?")
What's he doing? Exactly, he's left the class, he must be doing something. He didn't cease to exist! And your third, and most important question.
(waits for someone to say, "When's he coming back?")
WHEN'S HE COMING BACK! Yes! The keeping of a character offstage increases the impact of what we see onstage. The presence and absence of characters, the integration of onstage and offstage events, the creation of an atmosphere, a universe that collectively grips an audience with the fulfillment or frustration of expectations, we are invited to look ahead and to await. Minimizing the possibility of over-exposing the play's central figure, in this case, ME. All right. Now, finally, to complete today's scene.
(starts to get up from the chair, but halts and pauses)
How strange!

(pauses)

I just remembered a dream I had last night. I'm standing naked in the college fountain. Students are smiling and laughing. Blood. Blood is flowing out of me from a hundred wounds. Am I dying? Or perhaps giving life? No, I've been stabbed! But by whom?

(looks at the audience and realizes)

Oh, it was you.

"Beware the ides of March."

dee-Dum dee-Dum dee-DUM! Is that a request? Or a warning? Hmmm. We can make time. If that's where your interests lie.

"Beware the ides of March."

Shakespeare's most famous short line. Short lines are indeed an integral element of Shakespeare's verse technique. Most students ignore this feature. But apparently not my students.

"Beware the ides of March."

The verse, which might become static and predictable, suddenly turns terse, curt, swift, ominous, surprising. You'll remember it is the Soothsayer who states,

"Beware the ides of March."

But do you remember Julius Caesar's startled reply?

"What man is that?"

Merged together,

"Beware the ides of March, what man is that?"

dee-Dum, dee-Dum, dee-Dum, dee-Dum, dee-DUM! By completing the pentameter Caesar has attempted to neutralize the warning. But later in the play, Caesar, on his way to the Senate and potentially his destruction, again encounters the Soothsayer. The short line still hanging in the air. Caesar speaks arrogantly,

"The ides of March have come."

A short line, six syllables, three stresses. If the Soothsayer completes this pentameter, Julius Caesar may yet survive. We are attending a four-syllable short line with two stresses as a reply. Something like,

"The ides of March have come—And YOU are SAFE!"

No. There is no completion of the security-supplying pentameter. In fact Shakespeare, through the Soothsayer, will turn the verse on its head. We will now have two six-beat deviant short lines. Emerging from the verse the supernatural HEXAMETER! Listen for the terrifying metrical echo, as Caesar speaks, then the Soothsayer replies.

"The ides of March have come.

Ay, Caesar, but not gone."

Caesar is doomed.

(*pauses, then suddenly with surprise*)

But our scene! Don't look at me! Now you're forgetting today's scene!

(*gets the text from the desk, and looks at his watch with alarm*)

We're going to have to jump to late in today's scene where she demands murder, he refuses and she bids him farewell. May I have a couple of volunteers to read?

(*pauses, looks at the text and reconsiders*)

 Actually just a young woman, I'll play—

(*studies the text again for a moment*)

Well no, perhaps it would be more instructive for you if I play both roles. . . . The writing is in prose. Listen.

(*reads the first word from the text*)

"Now."

Did you catch the technique?

"Now."

The monosyllabic word! Perhaps no other Shakespearean technique is as expressive. Monosyllabic words convey emotional excitement. Again Hamlet is confronted with his father's ghost.

"Stay. Speak. Speak. I charge thee, speak!"

or, from *Coriolanus*,

"Kill, kill, kill, kill, kill him!"

Dum! Dum! Dum! Dum! Dum-Dum! Back to our scene. Wait, I'm sorry. It's difficult to play two different voices, and teach at the same time, especially in prose. Verse is actually easier for me. I'm better at verse. This is a gift that I have, and I am thankful for it. I know, let's go back a few scenes.

(*searches in the text turning pages*)

Ah, yes! The friar. He's speaking in verse. I'll play the friar. Hmmm. Yes. The friar, a deceptively significant role, often heavily cut, but in reality quite a challenge. He enters this other scene at a moment of absolute chaos and must, using only my voice, hush those present. Yes, here we go.

(*prepares a moment to speak, then proclaims*)

"Hear me a little for I have only been silent so long!"

(*stops*)

Let me just study the passage a second. We can make time for this.

(studies the passage a few moments, then looks up)

Perhaps I've told you this, but when I was in England, an assistant director, who had once witnessed a performance of the Royal Shakespeare Company, said I had the most perfectly developed classical voice. I traveled to all the great theatres, was seen by and impressed, well, everyone that would see me. My voice, my presence, my resonance, my projection. They all said I had the tools of a master thespian, the only thing my acting lacked was truth. "Suit the action to the word, the word to the action." That's all I couldn't do. I would always perform, even when I was unjustly refused an audition. I'd still, somehow, get in and perform. Sonnet 29, my specialty. In verse, of course, all sonnets are in verse. Do you know the sonnet? Ahh. I have a treat for you.

(puts text on table and gets chair, placing it down center)

Sonnet 29 is the first of the great sonnets. The first twenty-eight, not so much. Well, except for perhaps Sonnet 18. "Shall I compare thee to a summer's day." That one is great. Clearly. Sonnet 29 is the second great sonnet. But uniquely in this great sonnet, Shakespeare actually, for the first time, reveals himself. His profound depression and extreme discouragement. We think at the time of its writing Shakespeare's career is in jeopardy. Plague has closed the theatres. His wife and family miles away in Stratford. He is facing financial ruin. Fortune has indeed betrayed him. His life is spiraling downward, with a foreboding sense of alienation which threatens—well, I'd rather not explain it. I wish to perform it.

(stands like an auditioner announcing his next piece)

And I'm ready. Sonnet 29, by William Shakespeare. Oh, I will use a chair.

(sits then checks his diaphragm, he's ready)

"When, in disgrace with fortune and men's eyes,
I alone beweep my outcast state,
And trouble deaf heaven with my bootless cries,
And look upon myself and curse my fate—"

(suddenly stops)

Did I recite this last class? I believe I did. We're off track a little and I don't know why. Were you beginning to understand today's scene?

(pauses)

My wife left me recently. After she'd read your evaluations. "Wherefore was I to this keen mockery born?" I should have stayed in England. I was appreciated there. "Now I am alone." Well, don't feel so high and mighty. The only reason your evaluations are even considered is because the faculty wants me out! Shakespeare's my only friend.

    (*pauses*)

Shakespeare can be your friend, your advisor, your lover. He should be your God.

    (*pauses*)

Could someone bring me back to where I was?

    (*pauses*)

When I was a student in college one of my theatre professors suffered a breakdown in class. With tears streaming down his face, he went around the room hugging each of us individually. Looking deeply into each of our eyes, saying, "I love you, I love you, I love you." I'm not going to do that.

    (*pauses*)

How about a quiz? A quiz is definitely teaching! All right! A quiz. Yes. And I have one!

    (*stands*)

Can you identify verse from prose? It can be difficult as we just saw with the friar. Shakespeare's verse operates under its own authority, competing with powerful passages of prose and defying us to note the difference!

    (*puts chair back behind desk, and speaks with renewed energy*)

Verse or prose? Good, excellent, perfect, sublime. Shakespeare!

    (*suddenly lifts the chair and places it on top of the desk*)

The Winter's Tale, Act V Scene 3, a theatrical miracle! Verse or prose? Now remember, prose is the medium of servants and clowns. The ruling classes speak in verse. No serious love affair is pursued, no dangerous conspiracy is plotted, no royal ceremony is conducted, and no significant character dies, speaking in prose. On the other hand, no foreigner, no drunkard and no character suffering from an unbalanced psychology speaks in verse. The sane characters speak verse, the mad characters speak prose. However, there are exceptions. Here's the situation. Behold the statue of Hermione.

    (*points to the chair on the desk*)

Paulina commands the statue of Hermione to return to life and come down to Leontes. The lines you are about to hear are heavily punctuated and invite pauses everywhere? Verse or prose? Here it is:

"Music Awake her Strike! Tis time! Descend! Be stone no more. Approach!" Verse or prose? Certainly the appearance of prose, a staccato voice and a monosyllabic word, "Strike!" Verse or prose? . . . "I pause for a reply." There's only two choices. It is verse!

"Tis-TIME de-SCEND be-STONE no-MORE ap-PROACH!" dee-Dum, dee-Dum, dee-Dum, dee-Dum, dee-DUM!

(takes the chair down and puts it behind the desk)

All right, we are moving forward, covering material. NOW THIS IS TEACHING!!! Other things. The headless line, a line missing the initial unstressed syllable, signifying impatience. "Where the devil should this Romeo be?" "Where"—first syllable stressed. No dee-Dum, but "Dum!" All right, I am making sense! The broken-backed line lacks an unstressed midline syllable conveying an energetic shift in thought. "Horrible Sight! Now I see tis true." "Sight," "Now," together and stressed, the broken-backed line! Yes! Yes! We are on the road. Why are we on the road? Because I have the map! Get this down:

The unseen life offstage.

The unseen inner life.

The illumination of the inner mind through the onstage face.

The disruption of previously achieved balances of rational and irrational impulses.

The chosen self-image.

The displacement of libidinal energies into political action.

The inclusion of infantile experience to create present day conflicts.

Post-coital male disgust!

(pauses)

No, no, that's not in Shakespeare!

(suddenly struck with horror)

Oh my God, our scene, I'm forgetting today's scene!

(runs back to his text and searches for today's scene, desperately flipping pages)

Where is it? May I have a page number, please? May I have a page number? PLEASE?! Oh I see, you've no problem filling out negative evaluations, but I can't get a simple page number!

(if someone shouts out a page number at random, Dr. Keir will find the page called out, then realizing it's the wrong page, look at that person who shouted out the number and say)

Very funny.

(looks at his watch, stands frozen a moment, then continues)
"The inaudible and noiseless foot of time."

We won't be able to get through today's scene.

(retreats to his briefcase, starts to put away his things, but pauses, holding up his text and the evaluations)

You mustn't judge me unfavorably. I'm trying to inspire you with new insights. Cherished memories. The glory of words.

(holds up his text)

Do you know what it is to try and teach this? The infinity of things that may be studied in Shakespeare! It's not that I idolize, or go on tangents. I don't go on tangents, it's just that there's too much. Look.

(holds up the evaluations)

These student evaluations are "not generous, not gentle, not humble." Whatever we don't like we don't understand. Can't you understand my own evident enjoyment of the text. The music latent in the printed letters. I'm not a fraud as a—just give me another moment. Just. I know we're out of time! Here, here listen, a simple but pregnant line from . . .

(searches in his text)

King Lear! His last speech to his dying, already dead daughter Cordelia. The five times repeated "never." I'll play King Lear:

"Never, never, never, never, never."

Yes? Now you see? Suddenly we are aware that what to our ignorance seemed of little meaning, is simply charged with overwhelming significance. The unexpected beauty. And that's just one repeated word. Imagine trying to cover an entire Shakespearean scene in just one class. Oh, look at you, watching, evaluating, condemning. "Like flies to wanton boys, they kill us for their sport." Do you not realize what a single kind word would mean to me? No, of course not. I see your point. You're students, this is a class, if I don't teach it, clearly someone else will. Perhaps he or she will be to your liking. Perhaps he or she will complete the day's scene. Perhaps next time your evaluations won't destroy a marriage, a. . . If those of you who maliciously seek my destruction succeed and I am denied tenure, and forced off the faculty,

"I will have revenge on you all,

That all the world shall—I will do such things—
What they are yet, I know not, but they shall be
THE TERRORS OF THE EARTH!!!!!"
(*as he gestures with the folder of evaluations, the papers fly up and shower down to the floor; he stares at the mess before him and pauses*)
"When we are born we cry that we are come
to this great stage of fools."
Please. You absolutely must see this from my side.
(*gets on his knees and starts picking up the evaluations*)
You must see this from my side. Now I'm begging you. No. No. No begging.
"When beggars die there are no comets seen;
The heavens themselves blaze forth the death of princes."
No, I'm not saying I'm a prince, a king, a thane, a Caesar. I'm saying, I'm experiencing my emotions one at a time, in a very clear order. Oh, an idea just popped into my head. There's another one.
(*jumps up and searches in his text*)
Let me find it. Very quickly. Just give me this chance. Oh wait, here's a better one. My favorite one, oh boy. The tension between and that's where we mostly get it from. The point being, it must be so, because the opposite appears to be so. Yes? Give it to me in Latin! *Lucus a non lucendo.* Am I making good sense?
(*pauses*)
I'm sorry, I didn't mean to imply my wife leaving me was somehow your fault. These evaluations just confirmed her opinions. Like Lady Macbeth and Macbeth, who last appear together in Act 3 when the play still has almost a thousand lines to go, my wife and I have been drifting apart for some time. "The thane of Fife had a wife. Where is she now?"
(*pauses*)
I never became the husband . . . actor . . . teacher . . . I can't even complete the assigned scene.
(*now is in tears*)
"Is it not monstrous that this player here,
But in a fiction, in a dream of passion, could force . . .
What's Hecuba to him, or he to Hecuba,
That he should weep for her?"
(*gathers himself*)

What's in Shakespeare, we only half understand. Imperfectly interpret, speeches not deciphered, hardly telling verse from prose. With Shakespeare we stumble, we recover briefly, and are quickly lost again. That's why I—you see? It's Shakespeare, the nature of Shakespeare. It's the nature of life. We all stumble, but we do learn. We did learn here today. We learned about the meaning of

" . . . a poor player
That struts and frets his hour upon the stage
And then is heard no more."

(looks down dejectedly, notices something written on one of the student evaluations at his feet, bends down, picks it up)

I didn't see this one. I thought I'd read all of them. One of you wrote this.

(reads out loud from the evaluation)

"Dr. Keir is passionate about his subject. He's my favorite professor."

(looks at the audience, he is profoundly moved)

Thank you. I shall cherish this.

(pauses, then holds up his hand as if at church)

And, if another Messiah ever does come, he will be in Shakespeare's person. But for now. . .

(lowers his hand)

that's all we have time for. dee-Dum, dee-Dum, dee-Dum-dee-Dum-dee-DUM-dee . . .

(he opens and closes his hand with each "dee-Dum," finally ending with his hand stretching out)

(FADE TO BLACK)

Keir in *Teaching Shakespeare* (2000).

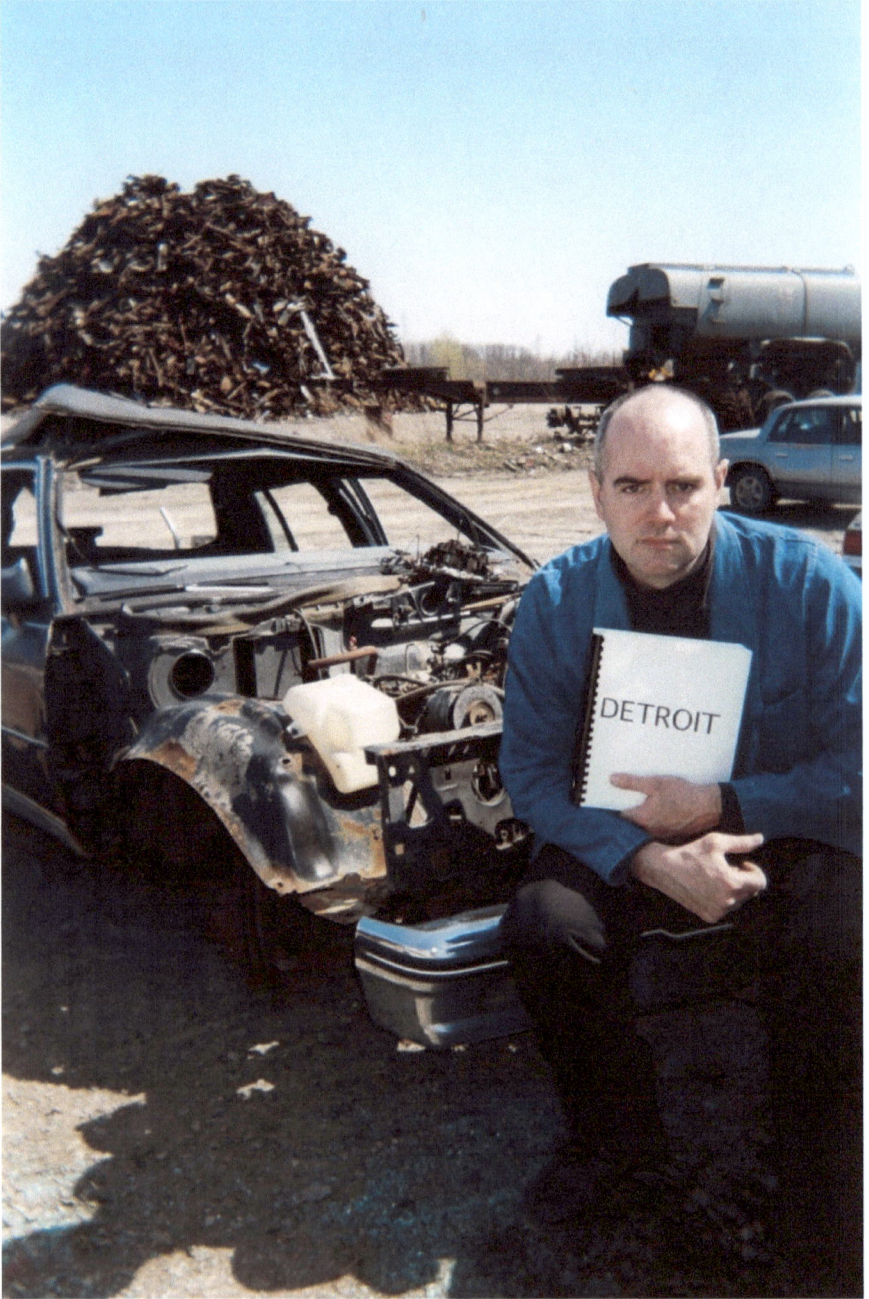

Keir in *Teaching Detroit* (2001).

ABOUT TEACHING DETROIT

Teaching Detroit, or *Teaching Shakespeare 2*, debuted at the 2001 Montreal Fringe Festival, played across Canada, was filmed and aired on Bravo!/Canada. Keir Cutler lived in Detroit in the 1990s. He was a theatre student at Wayne State University, where he earned an MA and a PhD.

Reviews:

"In this extraordinary sequel to last year's *Teaching Shakespeare*, Keir Cutler revisits his failed, narcissistic, alcoholic college professor on the edge of a nervous breakdown. . . . We laugh because, it's funny, because it's uncomfortable to watch an educated man dig his own grave, and because we're desperate to disavow the parts of us that identify with his failure." Erika Thorkelson, *See Magazine* (Edmonton)

"Cutler has laid claim to a unique vision, at once scholarly, riotous and irreverent, sort of like lit critic Harold Bloom with dick jokes." Matt Radz, *The Gazette* (Montreal)

"Keir Cutler struck gold with his character of a college teacher whose fascination with Shakespeare, mixed with his own inability to conduct a half-decent class, made *Teaching Shakespeare* a big hit with Fringe audiences across North America. . . . *Teaching Detroit* is no different." Kamal Al-Solaylee, *EYE Weekly* (Toronto)

"Cutler has constructed a great portrait in *Teaching Detroit*, one that combines equal parts of comedy and drama to bring a fully rounded character to life." Justin Bell, *Edmonton Sun*

"Cutler is the personification of every terrible teacher you've ever had—preening, condescending and prone to wild digressions. He's added his own unpublished semi-autobiographical novel, *Detroit*, to the course list, and that city's decline mirrors his own downward spiral." Jill Wilson, *Winnipeg Free Press*

"Burgeoning with taut language that overturns literary, theatre and teaching conventions, *Teaching Detroit* continues the story of its predecessor of last year, with Keir Cutler returning as a failed actor and writer condemned to teach in community college. . . . Cutler not only explores personal failure, but the failures of society to protect its more vulnerable as well, and does so with outrageous humour and offhand Shakespearean references. A must-see for all, especially all you unpublished novelists out there." Wayne Arthurson, *Vue Weekly* (Edmonton)

TEACHING DETROIT

(A classroom. Desk and chair. Carrying a briefcase, a water bottle with a yellow liquid, and a portable music player, DR. KEIR enters with a huge smile.)

DR. KEIR

Good morning! Good morning! Good morning! Today is a very exciting day! You know, I've looked forward to this class all term. One of the real joys of teaching here at community college is the liberty to add significant works to the curriculum. Today, we have reached, in our survey of world fiction, the class where we look at my novel.

(*takes his unpublished novel out of his briefcase*)

What an extraordinary opportunity for those of you here through our adult competency program. You did not finish high school. You have no degree or diploma of any sort, and yet today you find yourself in the presence of not only a teacher, but an unpublished author! Do you have any idea how overqualified I am for this job? I have also been an actor and a teacher of Shakespeare, and great at both. Shakespeare was the universal genius who received his themes from the divine. Well, those very themes are alive in this work. My work. My novel. Titled simply, *Detroit*.

(*reveals the cover of his novel with the word, DETROIT*)

But unlike Shakespeare, who never visited many of the cities and towns which were the settings for his plays, I actually traveled to Detroit! I went into a world, students, a dark, threatening world, and brought out this book. I implored you last class to purchase my book. I gave you a preview, a taste. I quoted Keno, the book's protagonist or antagonist, depending on how you interpret me in the novel. Yet instead of hearing your compliments and applause, all I've been hearing are your grumblings about the twenty-five-dollar price tag. Well, today that's about to change. Because after you've heard some more passages— passages that will leave you breathless—you'll race your fellow students down to that community college bookstore, praying there is still a copy available to you at any price!

(*opens the novel*)

I start the novel just after I was denied tenure and forced off the faculty at my former teaching position. My wife had left me at this point, but that didn't work as literature. So, in the book, I leave her. Because as protagonist or antagonist, I must be a man of action, and not entirely a victim. I tried to memorize the entire text, but I'm afraid I will have to read some of it. *Detroit*, chapter one.

> (*he dramatically reads the opening words*)
> "I have reached the ripe to rot age of 33. The age Jesus died on the cross. I have lost my job and become sexually impotent. Sit semi-conscious in front of the television, my wife accuses me of being a worthless failure who has never accomplished anything. A dark, paralyzing curtain of depression overwhelms me and I resolve to kill myself."
> (*stops reading*)

I have to pause a moment. Now I know many of you are new to literary criticism, and perhaps to books in general, but I've been told by editors that my death wish seems contrived. Do you know the definition of "contrived"? Artificial, forced, unnatural. And this somehow explains my novel's non-publication. Nonsense! When something is contrived, we feel safe and open to a more profound understanding. Write that down. Incidentally, yes, I could self-publish, but that is an affront to literature. A writer gets a publisher to publish his book. This is a great book! Egomaniacs self-publish, and I am nothing if not humble.

> (*reads*)
> "I have no plan how to kill myself. And am too sluggish and stagnant to follow through on any plan if I did. I am going to need help. My first thought, . . . Detroit, the murder capital. The most dangerous city in America. Perfect. I secretly load up my aging car in the middle of the night. No long goodbyes. Although one final failed attempt at an emotionally disconnected half-awake sex act with my wife from behind."
> (*again stops reading*)

Incidentally, the impotence is contrived to set up the spectacular climax that ends the novel.

> (*reads*)

"After the aborted sex, I pretend to fall asleep, quietly get up, sneak out of the house and am gone, to Detroit, Michigan. I arrive in late summer to find a barren, post-apocalyptic, urban ruin. This is the way the world ends, rats' feet over broken glass. America's sixth largest city leading the USA in virtually every negative statistic, including murder. I merely have to wander and wait, until my killer finds me. Perfect!"
(*stops reading*)

Okay, analysis. Where are we? Detroit! How do we know this? The title tells us. Who has taken us there? Me, the first person narrative. I have taken you. Not he, or they, or Huckleberry Finn for that matter. No, there is no such third-person distance. You and I are traveling together. And do we believe this story? Yes. Why? Because we believe in the place. Detroit. What would happen if we stepped into Detroit? What would happen if Detroit stepped into us? Listen.

(*reads*)
"I walk by brown fields of broken concrete, burnt out homes, a party store, rotting collapsed structures, mud lots, falling towers, another party store, a white cinder block medical clinic offering Detroiters money for their plasma. Whole city blocks overrun with bricks, tires, weeds, rust and rats. Street after street lined with roofless, windowless boarded up buildings, the fourteen-story Hudson's Department Store, once one of the largest retail establishments in the country, now dark, vacant, and flanked by empty, high rising erections fruitlessly reaching up into a brown fog. The perfect place to die!"
(*stops reading*)

Exciting, isn't it? This is the world-class writer at work at his most enthralling best. We are there! Joseph Conrad in the heart of the jungle. Herman Melville whaling on the open sea. Me in Detroit. Making connections, tie-ins, taking the present moment and connecting the dots. Life becomes literature. The world exists to become a book! A book, success! That's what this is about, reaching out into the world and grabbing success. Right here on these pages! Ah! Important question.

Why the impoverished inner city of Detroit? Because, as in Shakespeare, landscape always mirrors the hero's inner state. Detroit, wasted potential. The great actor-teacher-writer reduced to teaching dropouts. The great industrial city reduced to rubble. Detroit becomes character. We await what? Rebirth, Renaissance. The life-affirming phoenix, rising from the ashes of an urban wasteland, a work of art, a novel, rising out of the crumbling bricks of a failed professional and family life. The book, the writer, the city become one. Detroit, me, the distinction, invisible. ART AT THE PINNACLE!!!!!

> (*calms himself, then reads*)
> "I trudge on, searching this wasteland peppered with party stores."
> (*stops reading*)

Let me stop here. "Party store" is the Detroit name for a convenience store selling beer and liquor. Every block seems to have one. They look like military fortresses with huge steel doors, surrounded by fencing and razor wire. Inside, the black customers are separated from the staff by two-inch thick bulletproof glass. I originally had an explanation of "party stores." I explained the lack of black-owned businesses. But I cut it. Why? Because I got so-called "constructive feedback." "You're writing a novel, not a textbook." Isn't that one of the liberties of writing a novel? You can simply stop dead and explain or describe something, sometimes for several pages. I admit an explanation is unacceptable in many other literary forms. A theatre play, for example. You can't simply stop dead in a theatre play and say, "Oh, by the way, let me tell you about party stores."

> (*pauses*)

Well, I guess you're glad I cut the explanations. Put them back and the bookstore would have a stack of fifty-dollar novels waiting for you.

> (*flips through some pages and finds something he likes*)

Oh, here's an explanation that I left in. Listen to this, it'll give you a feeling for what the novel might have been.

> (*reads*)
> "Have you ever read a science-fiction novel set after the nuclear holocaust where the survivors live in the bombed-out

remains of civilization? That's Detroit. Whites had long since fled to the suburbs, white flight, and later prosperous, professional blacks had fled to the single integrated suburb of Southfield, black flight. Anyone who could get out of Detroit had. Even the great Motown Records, famous for recording Diana Ross and the Supremes, Marvin Gaye, the little Stevie Wonder, the Temptations, the Jackson Five, moved by its founder Berry Gordy all the way to Los Angeles, leaving yet another abandoned building in Detroit. It would take years before it would reopen as a museum."
(*stops reading*)

This is Shakespearean! The external setting reflects the internal mind. The abandoned teacher in the abandoned city. The macrocosm has indeed become the microcosmic. This is no incidental setting, students. And my book reads much better than it plays.

(*reads*)
         "And there he is! A pitch black emaciated skeleton of a man wearing an oversized black and silver Raiders coat like a giant swooping cape. I recognize him immediately. My Angel of Death."

(*stops reading, starts acting out the novel's conversation between an inner city black man and himself*)

         "'Hey fella, hey big fella, hey Chief! What you doin' down in Detroit?' I resolve to ignore his calls.
         'Hey My Man. HEY WHITE BOY!' I take my last long, full breath. I have determined my destiny. I am ready.
         'Someone call you? You a cop? Don't get no white dudes chillin'. You a cop!'
         'No, no, I'm a teacher. I'm not a policeman.'
         'Ah, for real? Straight up?'
         'Yes, really. Completely lost, all by myself. Do you understand?'
         'Say wut? By yoself, down in Detroit?'
         'That's right.'

39

'Ah, oh! Then you don't know nothin' 'bout Detroit. My name's Keno, man and Keno know Detroit.'
(*an aside*)

Keno—protagonist, antagonist—we don't know.

(*continues the conversation*)
'"Hold up! I see where you at. A teacher, huh? But you don't enjoy livin' round. That where Detroit come in. You got the book knowledge up here. But sometimes you wanna to step into the world to see if the book knowledge any good. Down in Detroit, you goin to see the prostitution, the dope, the robbin', the stealin', the killin', the dyin', every damn thing that's happenin'. You comin' into Detroit. You comin' into the world."'
(*stops*)

Okay! Very interesting. A failed impotent teacher with mental problems in suicidal despair, leaves his wife, goes in search of his death in Detroit. A wasteland peppered with party stores and danger. He spots Keno, whom he first sees as a killer. But—and this is a major surprise––Keno engages him in conversation. Even seems to understand this teacher. As readers we wonder, is Keno the angel of death or perhaps the angel of life? The Greeks call this *peripeteia*, we call it reversal!
(*pauses*)
Are you with me? Because I know this story, I don't need to tell it.
(*pretends everyone is with him*)
Good. I must tell you, I've been extremely well since I've taught here. Healthy! I've tried to stay away from Shakespeare, that's helped. I still suffer bouts of depression. But who doesn't?
(*picks up his novel and turns some pages*)
Hmm! All right, this is where it really slows down. Oh-oh-oh! Here. This is an interesting monologue. Well, more like a fragment. Doesn't work in the book, but out of context it absolutely sparkles. Again Keno.

(*reads*)
'"I love dis country. Mmm-hmm. It fucked up, true enough, have shitty buildin's with shitty dealin's and shitty

people livin' in 'em, but no place else in the world can you go and live like you can in United States. Say what you want, do what you want, kill how many motherfuckers you want and probably get off. Freedom is here. Welcome to Detroit.'"
(*stops*)

Did you notice my very creative use of the word "motherfucker"? It's throughout the novel. "Motherfucker" as a noun, synonymous with everything. Equally useful as an adjective, and most startlingly and this perhaps breaks new artistic ground. "Motherfucker" successfully conjugated as a verb, as in "Motherfuck you, bitch!" That's brilliant!

(*continues performing his novel*)
"Keno lives in the Willinghurst Hotel for Transients. A four-story dark brick building with no elevator that somehow survived the 1967 riots in Detroit, the largest act of civil disobedience in America up until that time. From the streets of Detroit came the cry, 'We goin' to make Vietnam look like a holiday!' Ten square miles with major fires. Entire city blocks in flames. And yet somehow this block with the Willinghurst survived. The perfect place to die, or perhaps to live. I rent a sparsely furnished room on the fourth floor of a building where the front door lock is always busted, even if it is repaired, it's busted by the following morning. A building where, thanks to the busted front door lock, there is continuous traffic in the halls all night, every night. Where thin four-inch metal tubes with one black burnt end are turning up everywhere, left in corners, on the stairs, by the front door, in the street gutter outside, like forgotten Easter eggs. And on every radio, tape player, stereo, boombox, always the same pulsating, throbbing song. MC Hammer's 'You Can't Touch This!'
(*sings*)
'Do-dododo-dodo.'"
(*explains*)

Okay, this song dates the novel. But if a publisher ever picks it up, I can change the song. I'm not one of those writers who thinks every word he puts down is untouchable, perfect and communicated directly from the divine.

(*continues from memory*)
    "And at my door, a daily parade of items always on sale
for five dollars, pots, pans, food stamp—'give me 50 cent on the
dollar, that's a ten dollar stack,'—telephones, radios, tape
players, kittens, puppies, law books, 'you into law, man? just
spot me five, they yours,'—charity packages of food, toiletries,
old magazines, footwear, clothes, all for just five dollars, even
auto parts, power tools, expired prescription drugs, and sex,
from Lina. An alluring teenager, wearing a t-shirt with the
printed phrase, 'Detroit, where the meek are killed and eaten.'
No make-up, hair a mess under a ragged, dark cap, absolutely
no attempt to be attractive, she arrives at my door offering me a
blowjob for just five dollars.
    'Ah, thanks, but I'm temporarily out of commission.'
    'Then can I get five dollars for some *ange* juice?'
    'Orange juice isn't five dollars.'
    'Oh, I only drink the good kind.'
    'Why is it always five dollars? What ever you want,
won't ten get you two? Or twenty get you four? Why is
everything always on sale for five dollars?' No answer. She
begins turning her cap in mesmerizing circles. Going round and
round."
(*circles his hand around his head a few times*)
    "Finally I speak.
    'Doesn't your arm get tired of doing that?'
    'Someone oughta put somethin' in my mouth.'"
(*suddenly stops*)

You know, a thought just hit me. I would not be standing here right
now reading my novel to you had I been a success. This job. This
classroom. You students. All represent my failure. It's taken me a long
time to face, but I'm so much healthier now that I refrain from dwelling
on my mistakes. It's not about the past or even the future. It's all about
now. Here, but here upon this bank and shoal of time at community
college. We still have judgment here. You see what I really wanted was
to be an actor, a Shakespearean actor. They're the only real actors. So I

went to England, but faced with rejection, I gave up, came back here. Got married, got divorced. Started this teaching thing. Which—yeah!
(with disgust, goes back to his novel and starts turning pages in frustration)
No. No. No.
(looks up)
I should have stayed in England. That was my mistake. If I could just somehow go back in time.
(suddenly launches into Shakespeare)
"Oh for a muse of fire, that would ascend the brightest heaven of invention, A kingdom for a stage, princes to act, And monarchs to behold the swelling scene. . . . Think when we talk of horses, that you see them, Printing their proud hoofs in th' receiving earth."
(acts out a horse stomping on the stage, gets carried away, eventually stopping himself in embarrassment)
Please. Please. Stop me when I . . . *Detroit*.
(goes back to his novel and again starts turning pages in frustration)
No. No. No.
(turns pages more violently, then looks up)
Are you still with me? Are you engaged? This is not easy for me, I could use your support. If I could feel something coming from you. This is like the difference between a white church and a black church. Well, at this moment, I feel I'm in a white church. Now that we're stopped, let me ask you something. How did everyone one of you know not to buy my novel? What do you have, some sort of extrasensory awareness? A collective intelligence? Or did someone pass the word? "Don't buy his novel. Don't buy it. He can't flunk all of us!"
(looks at some pages in his novel)
Nothing ever happens.
(pauses)
Do you know Michigan? Ever been to Michigan? Ever met anyone from Michigan? Ask them where in Michigan they're from. They'll go like this.
(holds right palm up)
You know what that is? Michigan. Yes. The Lower Peninsula of Michigan. It's the shape of a hand. Look on a map! You know what

43

they call this?

       (points to his thumb)

The thumb. Detroit is down here. You know what's below Michigan. South of Michigan? South of the United States of America? Canada. Yes. Yes. Yes! Michigan in United States is north of Canada. Yes, Canada sneaks a piece of Ontario right underneath Detroit. Strange, isn't it. Surprising. Arresting. The perfect place to set a novel. The world turned upside down!

       (turns his hand upside down)

Okay, so you're Canada.

       (points at audience)

Here's the Detroit River.

       (points at the space in front of the stage)

And this is Detroit.

       (points at the stage)

There's the all-white suburbs.

       (points upstage)

Warren, over 80% white, bordering on Detroit. Livonia, over 80% white, bordering on Detroit. And Dearborn, over 80% white, bordering on Detroit. And here's Detroit, over 80% black and impoverished. All right, back to my novel. It's night and we're outside the Willinghurst.

       (returns to acting out the novel)

       "On the stoop a small crowd of African-Americans, chain smoking cigarettes, passing around a brown bag of liquor. They drink and smoke in silence, listening to the hiss of sewer steam as it clouds the street, watching the beam from a Nightsun on a police helicopter lighting up some remote brick ruins. I have no will to wander, yet something leads me through the broken key door back into the dank mildew smell of the Willinghurst, past the smashed-in mail slots, everything in shades of brown, a flickering half-extinguished exposed fluorescent light, scurrying cockroaches over dark-stained, worn-brown threadbare carpet. The ground floor. Black military vets. Several of them. Army paraphernalia decorating each door. War photos, banners, spent shells, the black and white Missing In Action flag. From behind closed doors come monologues delivered to no one. These vets have exchanged an overseas war zone for an American one, and now many suffer frequent flashbacks, sending them diving to the floor or even out the window. A ground floor room reduces the fall. Up a staircase. Angry banging and shouts. Oh, look, there's Keno stabbing a long piece of metal into a solid, though splintering door. Keno is bleeding from the mouth, demanding entrance and revenge for some earlier offence."

(*acts out Keno slamming a metal pipe into a door*)

"'Motherfuck you, bitch!' I smile politely and proceed by.

'Hey, Keno, busy?' More doors, a screaming baby, then an argument, then music, 'do-dodo-do dodo,' then a room with no door but steel bars with someone visibly sitting, waiting inside.

'What *cha* need, man?'

'Thanks, I'm set.'

Up another staircase, and a grammatically incorrect message, carved graffiti style into a wall, 'It not the Willinghurst, it the Killinghurst.' The Killinghurst! The third floor, more doors, 'do-dodo-do dodo, Can't touch this!'"

(*pauses*)

"Then Lina's voice and the sounds of sex. I listen."

(*pauses*)

"Jealousy pushing my ear against the door, possessiveness to anger, to, to, to, arousal, I'm getting an . . . I'm getting an . . ."

(*looks down at his crotch, then quickly looks up*)

"Oh, people in the hall! I pull away from the door, nod a greeting, pretending nonchalance.

'Yo, wut up?'

I hustle back to my fourth floor room, too late, the erection is gone. Late that night, there is a soft, almost imperceptible knocking, a knocking at my door. 3 AM. An assassin! Has to be. This is it. I go to the door. I open it."

(*mimes opening a door, then closes his eyes, grimacing, expecting to be shot; after a moment, opens his eyes*)

"It's Lina. She's carrying a beat-up tape player. She wants five dollars for it.

'You ain't got no music. No music, no party. What if yo' want to bust out and dance. What yo' gonna do? Ain't worth livin' 'round wit' no music.'

'First of all, I don't want to live . . . around. And I don't dance. I can't dance. I feel awkward, self-conscious.'

'Ain't nobody born can't dance. Dance the runnin' man. You can run yo' can dance. I put it on, yo' see. Just run where yo' at.'

'Run, to the music, that sounds easier than dancing.' I try. But Lina stops the music.

'That not the runnin' man. That the stompin' cockroach man! Here watch me. I teach you.'"
(*starts music player and does the running man, dancing around the desk, then stops the music*)

"'Are you kidding? I could never do that.' I go to Lina, pull up 'The Meek are Eaten' t-shirt exposing her braless breasts. Exploring hands encounter no defense. She pushes me back, undoes my belt and zipper. Exposing my limpness."
(*undoes his pants, which drop to the floor, exposing his underwear*)

"'No, no don't push me, I haven't, I need, I take . . . time. I need time.' Lina gets up and says, 'Work on yo runnin' man.' And she is gone."
(*now standing with his pants down around his ankles*)

Okay, analysis!
(*realizes his pants are down, pulls up his pants, zips the zipper, and continues*)
Two sexual situations, one the beginnings of an erection through voyeurism, the other limpness in reaction to human contact. Take special note. This, arguably the culmination of modern fiction!!! It's a brilliant piece of work. It's equal to anything we've looked at in this course. Not a word out of place. Not a word can be touched. Divine flawless perfection! You see why I had such high hopes for my novel? I envisioned it being taught everywhere. Teachers around the globe cracking open *Detroit*. Investigating its inner meaning. But I was stigmatized after being denied tenure. No four-year college or university wanted me, let alone my book. All that was left was

community college. And everyone's advice, "Stay away from community college. You'll never ever get back to university level."
(*pauses*)
And they were right. I'm alone now. Always alone. The young girl students don't come around anymore. Why is that? I always thought, you know as you get older, that father thing. I spent New Year's Eve alone. I've spent the last, well since my wife left, they've all been alone. But this last one went so much better. Instead of making some feeble attempt with a bottle, a solitary countdown, ten, nine, eight, whoopee! No. This New Year's I watched a film. At about eleven. Something about the end of the world. When I looked at my watch, it was 1 AM. New Year's was over. So much better. Did you have a good New Year's Eve? They never really are, are they? Good? No. Never.
(*looks at his watch, runs to his novel, and finds his place*)
Oh Jesus, my novel!

(*returns to acting out*)
"It's the following early evening. Keno arrives with a question.
'What wrong wit yo', Man? Ho outside tell me, yo' refuse a blowjob for just five dollars. Yo' can hold out on dem hoes awhile, but 'ventually you give in, you get sucked like you never sucked, yo' willie just go "POP!" Damn, like "POP!"'
Lina and her spinning cap begin popping in my mind. Keno pulls out a lighter, a thin metal tube, and a plastic vial with what looks like a crumbling sugar cube.
'What is that?' I ask.
'Paradise, man. Best shit that ever happen. Crystalled up 'caine. Don't know who figured it out. Better than the hair-on, cuz no needle. And no jones like wit' the hair-on. And it cheap. All yo' ever got in yo' mind is the next one of these.
'That's what all of you buy with five dollars??!!!'
'For yo' it's probably ten.' Keno lights the cube on the end of his metal straw and in one long breath it crackles and sparks and then disappears in smoke up the improvised pipe leaving a black burnt end. He holds his breath, then exhales, instantly becoming calm, spiritually calm. His eyes take on a gentle glassy texture and he smiles contentedly.

47

'Hey man, yo' know 'bout Devil's Night?'

'Devil's Night, no, what's that?'

'Ah, man, no Devil's Night where you from? Night 'fore Halloween. Devil's Night.'

'Oh, Mischief Night. Yeah, when I was a kid, we'd steal neighbors' doormats, throw autumn leaves inside unlocked cars, toilet paper a tree, we called it Mischief Night.'

'Well in Detroit it Devil's Night. Everybody leave out they house, try'n burn down da city! Trippin' out on mescaline, angel dust, little weed. Start setting fires all over. A house, don't matter. Sometimes abandoned, sometimes it be whole apartment buildin' with motherfuckers livin' in it. Set a fire, run like hell. Everybody just haul ass. Set a couple of mo, then backtrack and go check out the fire department, while they tryin' to put the motherfucker out. Big assed fires, blazin' out of control! In the thick of it all. Trip out over the way the flames be jumpin' 'round. The colors. Shapes that come up in it, like animals. Cats, dogs, horses. Devil's Night fun. There be so much smoke around, it look foggy outside. Hundreds, hundreds of fires. A whole city party.'

I stand beside Keno at my window. In the distance I can hear sporadic gunfire. In the window directly across, three small black faces. Three preschool children locked in a back room with, as far as I can see, nothing that they can create mischief with. No toys, no dolls, no crayons, no books, nothing! They slowly disappear in the twilight. Standing motionless until they see me. Then their eyes light up and huge smiles spread across their faces. They try to engage me in an impromptu game of peekaboo. I step away from the window and jump back into view. And it might as well be Christmas morning. Keno puts an affectionate arm around my shoulders. What a revitalizing dreamscape for a suicidal teacher escaping his limp past in the bourgeoisie or as it's known in Detroit, 'the Boogie Wazzie.'"
(*stops reciting*)

Okay. Analysis. The destructiveness of Detroit has become, in a sense, life affirming. It's engaging isn't it? My novel, even if it is contrived, well, perhaps "engaging" is too strong a word? But there is something.

And yet it remains unpublished. And there's history. Not just fiction. Listen to this.

(*acts out more of the novel*)
"The fifth of January 1914—to prevent an organized labor force, a major announcement comes out of Detroit. 'Ford Motors, the most successful automobile manufacturing company, will initiate the greatest revolution ever known to the industrial world. The Five-Dollar Day!' Five dollars a day more than doubles the current wage rate in America. Henry Ford sends recruiters to the U.S. South. Southerners are seen as docile labor, unlikely to unionize, and easy to recruit with the five-dollar-a-day promise. This is the start of the great northern migration of blacks and whites that transplants the south to the north. And also transplants the Ku Klux Klan. In just twenty years, KKK membership in Michigan runs into the hundreds of thousands, and is the largest of any state in America. Let me repeat that. The largest of any state in America. Not Alabama, Georgia, or Mississippi, but Michigan! These racist whites create "neighborhood improvement associations" to harass and terrorize blacks attempting to move into white areas. The blacks are kept crowded into a small ghetto euphemistically called 'Paradise Valley.' Where black tenants pay the highest rents for the most miserable housing. And are kept entirely out of wealthy Pointes east, Grosse Pointe, Grosse Pointe Farms, Grosse Pointe Woods, Grosse Pointe Shores, Grosse Pointe Park! As if a curse from God, the Dutch elm beetle descends on Detroit killing all the city's trees. Years of police brutality, poor housing, lack of jobs, blacks always being the last to be hired and the first to be fired. Henry Ford accepts the Iron Cross from Adolf Hitler!"
(*does the Nazi salute, lowers his hand, and turns to look at it; reminding everyone of the Lower Peninsula of Michigan, he is impressed with himself*)

Brilliant. Easily as good as Steinbeck! Yet publishers won't publish my novel. It makes no sense. Especially when it would mean so much to me.

(pauses)

You didn't answer me. Why haven't you all bought my novel? It's some sort of plot between you. All of you. To torture me. "Like flies to wanton boys." That's what teachers are. That's what I am.

(pauses)

I teach you well! And I don't go on tangents. Okay, perhaps, for a fiction course, I reference Shakespeare a little too much. But am I incoherent or unplanned? Never. Today we cover my novel, that's a plan. And the occasional tangent. Well, all of life is a series of tangents. Don't we just grip on to something, some idea of ourselves and run with it? An actor. I am an actor. A Shakespearean actor. I'm off to England. For a month, a year, a moment. Then suddenly the road ends. We stop. Uncertain. Despairing. Lost. But as if we've known all along, another road appears. A novelist. I am a novelist. I write novels! Yes this is me. This tangent is me. The real me. And we're off again. For another . . . until this road ends . . . in rejection! And finally our little life is rounded with . . . *Detroit*.

(pauses)

Okay, that's it. We're done. Go and do whatever it is you do when you are not here. Neck in the halls. Smoke your pot. Oh no, what is it now? Hardware store products. Go and sniff your hardware store products. You can go. I'm done with you. Class dismissed!

> *(raises his novel, high over his head with both hands and then throws it down violently on the floor, goes and sits behind his desk, takes a long drink; after a moment he looks out at the audience)*

I am so fed up with slinking into this class with my pocket full of breath mints and my vodka-diluted lemonade. Oh, what are you going to do? Report me? If they started firing alcoholic teachers, who'd be left to teach?

> *(stands up, and confronts the class)*

Let me tell you something. Today I was actually going to wait until after class. Go back to my office and celebrate. Celebrate for one day, one class. I was an artistic success.

> *(looks down at his novel on the floor, runs at it, kicking it to the side of the stage; he then walks toward it, takes a drink, and forces a stream of liquid through his teeth at it)*

There is a certain freedom to not giving a flying fuck.

(*suddenly puts his bottle down, runs and picks up his novel*)

I'm sorry, I really do need you to buy my novel. I sort of put myself in the hole. I was in debt to start with. Well, you understand. We're all adults here. You know what it is to make ends meet. I was really counting on . . . what am I going to do with fifty unsold copies? Please, please, if you could possibly help me out. I'd be happy to sign anyone's copy. All right, you don't have a so-called "solid educational background," okay we accept that, but you have "life experience," you must recognize, deep down, that I have something very valuable to teach And you've been wonderful about listening to me today, even if my novel is over your heads. Look, let's jump ahead. To the climax. It's spectacular. And life-affirming. And truth be told, the middle chapters sag. But the climax. Few people have ever got that far.

(*pauses*)

Synopsis. What happens in my book is Keno is revealed to be a violent drug addict with a heart of gold. Lina is revealed to be a prostitute drug addict also with a heart of gold. The Me character has begun to see the first flickers of light slit through his curtain of suicidal depression. Plotwise, there is a tragic murder and a comic drug bust. Everyone, including me, is evicted from the Willinghurst, now sardonically known as the Killinghurst. And there are a lot more descriptions of abandoned buildings. Okay, the climax!

(*reads*)

"I have been evicted from the Killinghurst. I am packing my things, when Lina appears.

'Keno got that Aids shit, he sick.'

'What? No more Keno, no more Killinghurst. It's impossible to get killed in this town.'

'Killed? Why you always wanna be gettin' killed? Death come soon enuf. Might as well party a little, while you livin' 'round.'

'It doesn't look like I've got a choice.'

Lina smiles, I smile back. She begins turning her cap. I ignore her suggestive cap twirl and ask, 'Are you hungry, Lina? Could I buy you lunch?' We leave the Killinghurst for the last time and go and eat Coney Islands, hot dogs with meat chili and a zigzag of disturbingly bright yellow mustard. After lunch she shows me another transient hotel, on the other side of the block from the Killinghurst. She brings me to a room and inside three small children. The same three small children I play peekaboo with. They're hers! I move in with Lina and the children. And Lina gives up crack and selling herself. I read to the children every day. And every night we teach the children dancing. Lina does the runnin' man while I do the stomping cockroach. Halloween time comes. And I've forgotten my quest to die in a blaze of glory. Holding hands, we enjoy the Devil's Night fires from the building's roof. In early November word comes that Keno is dying. We bring him requested cigarettes on his deathbed. He has lost what flesh he has and is now just bones and skin. Too weak to smoke, Lina holds a cigarette to his lips. He manages a small puff then a smile then in a faint whisper he counsels, 'Enjoy livin' 'round. Enjoy livin' 'round.'

But I've heard of a new Aids hospice with a revolutionary therapy, we bring Keno there just in time and he begins to recover! And on New Year's Eve, when every Detroiter who can get his or her hands on a gun goes outside at midnight and fires off multiple rounds, I finally make love to Lina, not sex, love! Under heavy blankets with the windows thrown open, panting vapor, hearing the celebratory gunshots. Like the sound of popcorn at first, then building to a midnight crescendo far beyond the capacities of the human ear. A crackling, static-like auditory extravaganza. Tens of thousands of guns shooting simultaneously; creating one of the most extraordinary acoustic experiences on earth. A whole city party."
(*pauses*)
　　　"The end."

(*pauses*)
Listen, I'm thinking of having the bookstore reduce my novel's price. To ten dollars. Would that be acceptable? Next week is our Hemingway week, and that novel's no longer required. You don't have to buy it, buy mine. What do you say? Look, I know what it's like to be a student. Lectured at. It's like being held hostage. Victimized by the

psychological idiosyncrasies of your teacher. That's why I stick so strictly to the course material. What-what-what-*Detroit* is. *Detroit* is life-affirming. And I want all of you to have a copy. So, how about five dollars? Understand five is my absolute, not even breakeven, point. So what do you say? Five dollars. I can't go any lower than this.

(FACE TO BLACK *** *or there is an alternate ending which involves an additional actor and continues from the above*)

(*suddenly we hear a voice from the audience*)

KEVIN
I'll buy one.
(*a student, KEVIN, stands in the audience, comes to the front, takes out a five dollar bill, and hands it to DR. KEIR; KEVIN receives the copy of the novel from DR KEIR*)

DR. KEIR
. . . I'm sorry. . . . I forgot your name.

KEVIN
Kevin.

DR. KEIR
(*DR. KEIR is extremely touched*)
Thank you, Kevin.

KEVIN
Sure.
(*starts to return to his seat with the novel*)

DR. KEIR
Oh, Kevin, may I sign it for you?

(FADE TO BLACK)

ABOUT TEACHING AS YOU LIKE IT

Teaching As You Like It, or *Teaching Shakespeare 3*, debuted at the 2006 Montreal Fringe Festival. It was directed and dramaturged by TJ Dawe, and toured several Canadian fringe festivals. The monologue was selected to be performed at both Montreal's Wildside Festival, and the Uno Festival in Victoria, B. C.

Reviews:

"Excellent . . . a darkly satirical work." Pat Donnelly, *The Gazette* (Montreal)

"Utterly superb! . . . This is probably one of the funniest, darkest and most intelligent one-man plays to be found at the Fringe this year." Paul Gessell, *Ottawa Citizen*

"In *Teaching As You Like It* Dr. Keir is that saddest of figures on the academic totem pole—the high school substitute English teacher. . . . Dr. Keir is hilarious . . . Yet at the end, you don't know whether to laugh or cry. Don't miss this one." Colin MacLean, *Edmonton Sun*

"The Montreal actor takes *As You Like It* and turns its subject matter into a wildly hilarious and gripping one-man play. . . . a tight script that is pure comedy with a note of seriousness—not to mention an ending that will give you chills. Cutler has already established himself as one of the Fringe circuit's most entertaining and intriguing performers." Stephanie Classen, *Saskatoon StarPhoenix*

"The lines between reality and fantasy quickly blur as we're bewitched, bothered and sure, occasionally bewildered, savouring every minute. . . . Directed by the estimable TJ Dawe, solo outings at the Fringe don't get much better than this." Alan Kellogg, *Edmonton Journal*

"Magnificently sleazy." Gaetan Charlebois, *The Gazette* (Montreal)

"A tight script. A riveting performance." Amy Barratt, *Montreal Mirror*

"*Teaching As You Like It* is brilliant, intellectual humour that stimulates without patronising, engages without resort to cheap theatrics. Cutler's mastery of the one-man show is unparalleled, as he demonstrated once again this year to his captivated audience/students/fellow 'players.'"
Leila Marston, *Winnipeg Onstage*

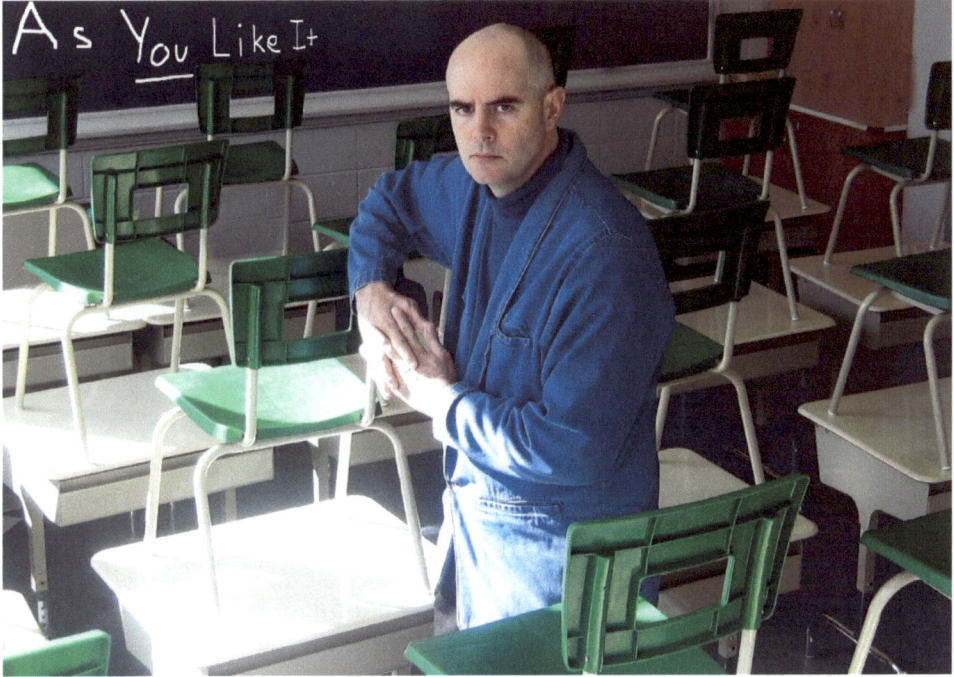

Keir in *Teaching As You Like It* (2006).

TEACHING AS YOU LIKE IT

(*Lights up on a high school class. A desk and a chair. DR. KEIR is standing, taking attendance. He is holding a binder with a pen. On the desk is a copy of* As You Like It.)

DR. KEIR

Francis, Chris, Edward, Bill, Bill, take off the iPod.
    (*mouths "take off the iPod"*)
. . . I'm sure you were listening to some Shakespeare . . . Mary, Sidney, Herbert, Ros?
    (*appears surprised that one of his students is not present*)
Is Rosalind Green here? Did anyone notice if Rosalind was in homeroom? How about the guys? I remember high school, all those overactive hormones. Did any of you guys take female attendance? No? Oh that's right, Rosalind is one of the few remaining girls who comes to school wearing something resembling decent clothing. Making her invisible. Guys, just a hint for later in life. It's up here that counts.
    (*taps his head*)
Well, it looks like we have a few stragglers, and I'm certain Rosalind is coming. She wouldn't want to miss our first day of *As You Like It* and Shakespeare's Rosalind. If today we were starting our look at *Coriolanus* and my name was Coriolanus, I'd be here. So why don't we wait a few before we dive into our class, our play, our comedy, our . . .
    (*trails off, sits behind desk and absentmindedly whistles*
    "Alouette," then he thinks of something)
Oh incidentally, while we're waiting, I don't believe I ever told you, in all my personal Shakespearean adventures, I once did perform in today's play, *As You Like It*. Thirty years ago, a college production, I was the lead, Orlando. Perhaps I didn't tell you because I was dreadful. I freely admit it. Hated the role. Even great actors can't play everything. All that silly prancing through the forest attaching banal love poems to trees. "O Rosalind. Sweet Rosalind." Shakespeare's male lovers are limp wristed wimps! But back then, I looked the part. I remember standing center stage during the play's opening monologue.
    (*stands and moves to center, positions his feet like a*
    classical actor)
I could never figure out what to do with my hands. The feet were fine.

(recites opening line of As You Like It, *with hands clearly out of sync with his words)*

"As I remember, Adam, it was upon this fashion bequeathed me by will but poor a thousand crowns, and, as thou sayest, charged my brother on his blessing to breed me well. And there begins my sadness."

(stares at his hands)

That's why I'm not a famous actor. It's because of my hands. They're always THERE. You don't think about them in real life. But when you get on stage suddenly there are these two claws, and wherever you put them seems to be the wrong place.

(moves his hands around trying to find a comfortable spot for them)

I was always watching them, my hands, that was my biggest fault by far—no, no, second biggest.

(drops his hands to his sides)

Listening to myself, that was my biggest. I'd listen to myself as these rehearsed, memorized lines, written by someone else, for someone else, were coming out of my mouth. And when it's Shakespeare you can't help doing a British accent. And of course because you're on stage, you're feeling absolute terror, because people are watching. And judging. Making you more self-conscious. So you're not paying any attention to what you're saying. The words are coming out, like a laundry list or telephone numbers with a fake accent. Your hands are sawing the air. And Orlando is supposed to be in love! The review in my college paper said I "failed to project the lovesick despair of a man longing for the consummation of the ideal love." That wasn't my fault! I tried to feel "lovesick"! I'd heard of method acting! I'd heard of Marlon Brando! I knew I was supposed to feel it! I even tried to develop a crush on the lead actress playing Rosalind. But we had no chemistry. Every performance I was dying for the final wedding scene to finally marry her and get the hell off stage.

(pauses)

And there was this all this construction on campus. I remember. Round the clock construction. There was some giant rush on to demolish some building beside the theatre. So throughout the show you could always hear jackhammers. Slightly muffled jackhammers, but jackhammers.

(pretends to be using a jackhammer, and makes the noise of one)

Everyone was irritable. On stage, backstage. Bickering, snapping, arguing. The cast detested one another. If only we had been doing a bloody and hate-filled tragedy like *Richard III* or *Titus Andronicus*. The audience was made up of parents, relatives and students who were all obligated to be there. And they were all looking at their watches. Every time I scanned the audience everyone was intensely consulting their watches. Like they were "dividing each minute into a thousand parts." But no one was asleep! Thanks to the jackhammers.

(*jackhammers again*)

Except my father. Who was snoring. In the front row. He came to every performance, to support me, but slept. And every time his snoring would get louder than the jackhammers, my mother, who also came to every performance, would elbow him in the ribs. And he'd wake briefly, consult his watch, then fall back to sleep. And I remember I was wearing these disgusting green leotards, and ballet slippers, and this rainbow colored, puffy Elizabethan codpiece designed to draw all visual attention, at all times. A matching a puffy shirt and really greasy makeup and sticky hair spray, and crooked eyeliner and lip gloss and rouge. And, and—

(*looks towards the classroom door*)

Well, it looks like Rosalind's not coming. Hope she's all right.

(*pauses*)

Okay, let's start then. Today's class. William Shakespeare's *As You Like It*. A very interesting play. But where to start?

(*flips through some pages*)

Hmm, how about starting with the most famous line in all of Shakespeare, which happens to be in *As You Like It*. I know, I know, when we were studying *Hamlet*, I said the most famous line in Shakespeare was in *Hamlet*. But as a rule the most famous line in Shakespeare is always in the particular play you happen to be looking at. So, can anyone tell me the most famous line in all of Shakespeare? From *As You Like It* . . .

(*waits for someone in the audience to yell out, "All the world's a stage"*)

"All the world's a stage!" So true! And "All the world's a stage!" is? a? meta? . . .

(*puts up four fingers*)

Four. "Metaphor." Very good. And "All the world's like a stage" is a . .

. "simile!" This is education! Now does Shakespeare say all the world is *like* a stage? No. The world's not like a stage. The world *is* a stage. It is a stage. Metaphors are strong. Similes are weak. And Shakespeare is never weak. Unless he consciously decides to be weak. Which he does from time to time. And in these cases he uses similes. But "All the world's a stage" is more than a metaphor. More than a comparison. It is a statement of fact. A statement that we are all on stage. And whether we like it or not, we must all perform! Why? Because "all the world's a stage and all the men and women merely players." Players? Hockey players? No. Players are actors. We are all actors. And, according to Shakespeare, "merely actors." Merely meaning, "nothing more." All the world's a stage and we are nothing more than actors. Shakespeare telling us we're not human beings determining our own destinies. We're actors following some preordained script. Life is not a self-creation. Shakespeare doesn't say all the world's a stage and all the men and women playwrights. And why doesn't he? Because we're not. Playwrights. We're actors. And what does it really mean to be an actor?

>   (*pauses*)

It means we have absolutely no control over our lives. An actor playing, say, Othello doesn't one night strangle Desdemona in a fit of paranoid jealousy, then the next night realize he's jumped to a totally false conclusion and live happily ever after with his beloved wife. Afraid not. An actor strangles Desdemona night after night after night, over and over and over. He can't do anything else. Character is destiny and destiny is character. How many times have I repeated this basic rule of Shakespeare, this basic rule of life? Take me. I'm not a teacher. No. Well, yes, yes, I'm a teacher. But in reality, according to Shakespeare, I am an actor playing a teacher. This isn't a classroom, this is a stage! And you're not students, you're pretending to be students. And I didn't even give you a choice. So, "All the world's a stage and all the men and all the men and women merely players. They have their entrances and their exits and one man in his time plays many parts." Bullshit! Sorry to swear in front of young minds, but Shakespeare has made a mistake. I never state Shakespeare's made a mistake, but here he's made a mistake. An error of gargantuan proportions. "One man in his time plays many parts"? No. One man in his time plays one part. The same part. Over and over. And over. Again take me, I seem to have a recurrent difficulty holding on to my teaching positions. Over and over again, I lose them. At the university, thanks to envious professors who feared my talent and knowledge, I was denied tenure and forced off the faculty, sinking first downward to community college to teach dropouts, where I understandably developed a drinking problem, and was let go, and now plummeting down, down, down, ever downward in absolute free fall, not unlike Lucifer tumbling from paradise, to here, to high school, and a substitute English teacher. Can there be anything lower? As Touchstone himself might have said, "Now I am in high school, the more fool I, when I was in university I was in a better place."

(*pauses*)

I was so looking forward to Rosalind being here today. You probably noticed she's one of my favorites. Teachers have favorites, we all know that's inevitable. I wonder why she?—Perhaps, like her Shakespearean namesake in *As You Like It,* Rosalind has run away to the safety of the forest? To live an uncorrupted, simple life in rural tranquility far from the wicked, sinister, malevolent city. You think that's it?

(*pauses*)

Is there anyone that knows why Rosalind is not here? Look, I know I am just a substitute but I have been here for a couple of months since your regular teacher, Mr. Devere, fell sick and was unable to perform what you've suggested was his perfunctory, uninsightful race through some of Shakespeare's plays, thus bringing me here. I haven't asked you for anything up until now but your attention, which is the most valuable thing you own. I've entertained you with my sonnets and soliloquies, tried to bring the works to life. Tried to make Shakespeare something other than an interminable, incomprehensible torture that your regular teacher is apparently famous for, BUT will put me back out on the street once his health, God bless him, returns. Now will someone please answer this question: Has anyone had any sort of contact from Rosalind—Rosalind Green—this morning? Email? Voicemail? Text message? Carrier pigeon? This is ridiculous, she hasn't missed a class since I've been here, and today she's absent, and on the day when we begin our look at her play. And make no mistake, *As You Like It* is Rosalind's play. Oh, there are other characters. Other luminous characters. But the play, like almost all of Shakespeare's plays, is based on another work, *As You Like It* is based on a book by Thomas Lodge, titled *Rosalynde.* So it would have been nice if the real, flesh and blood, Rosalind were here. Okay, that's enough, we're going to stop!

(*sits behind desk*)

Stop pretending. Pretending we all don't know what's really, actually going on. Here. In this classroom, on this stage. I'm not fooling you. And you certainly aren't fooling me. Yes, I have heard the rumor. The rumor circulating throughout this high school. *Vis a vis* a certain overqualified substitute and a certain now absent student. More precisely, "the evil lecherous teacher, me, and the naive innocent child-student, Rosalind." That's your rumor, isn't it? Well, I will not dignify such a preposterous insinuation with a denial.

(*pauses*)

Nothing has gone on . . . Nothing! The rumor, if there is a rumor, is a lie. A lie that, given Rosalind's absence from class today, perhaps even she's begun to believe. Being at an impressionable age. But not so impressionable that she is not old enough to make informed consent. If she ever decided to do such a thing. Which I don't think I'm giving away any secrets here, she may have already done with some of the more randy young gents in our fair academy—which is entirely legal and none of my business—except for the fact that it is my understanding that I am being victimized by a malicious rumor. And please notice I am very calm about this. You see my conscience is at peace. I know it's unlikely that I'm likely to have done anything . . . unpleasant . . . with Miss Green. So I can just sit here like the forested characters in *As You Like It* and "fleet the time carelessly."

(*pauses, then again whistles "Alouette"*)

Teaching is one of the most basic human relationships.

(*pauses*)

I operated in good faith and solely for Rosalind's benefit.

(*pauses*)

The majority of student-teacher liaisons are swept under the rug. That's all I ask—treat me like the majority. All right. All right. If nothing happened between Rosalind and me, I'm sure you're wondering what did happen. And why isn't she here? On her day? Your classmate Rosalind Green and I have had . . . a trust-based relationship. I'm not one of those know-it-all superior, pompous professors who lords over everyone his exhaustive knowledge. I'm warm, and friendly, and approachable. I have rapport . . . with certain students. And having rapport is paramount to teacher-student interaction. So Rosalind and I were candid with each other. And that's where this . . . rumor is from. She related her previous relationships. I related my sorry tale of broken hearts, mine, over and over. And at times—and this was my mistake, my only mistake in this minor misunderstanding—at times I sought her approval and guidance. In the emotional state I've been in. No wife, no girlfriend, reduced to high school substitute teaching, for Christ's sake! So yes, Rosalind and I had the odd conversation outside class. That's it. That's all.

(*pauses*)

And let's remember, every Rosalind, fictional or otherwise, needs her young, gorgeous athletic masculine specimen, Orlando, conquering wrestlers, killing lions and defeating poisonous snakes. As you can plainly tell, I'm no longer Orlando. So the devilish rumor of intimacy doesn't quite fit. Instead, if anything, I'm like Jaques. If you've done your homework and read the play you now know the cynical, black view of life, "all the world's a stage," Jaques, "who can suck melancholy out of a song, as a weasel sucks eggs." Jaques is the only entirely contemplative character in all of Shakespeare. The only one. He thinks and does NOTHING. The perfect professor. A gawky, badly dressed, bookish, unkempt, constantly embarrassed, accustomed to being excluded, balding, brainy, totally lacking in appeal, Jaques! That's me! No one will ever believe Rosalind fell, even momentarily, for a Jaques. Ergo, I am in the clear! Ha! And I repeat, nothing happened! Okay? We're clear, we're clear? The rumor is over. It's over. It's over. We're clear! We're clear. It's over. Finally. Thank you.

(*takes a very deep breath*)

That's a relief. Now will you stop pestering me with this and allow me return to today's play?

(*gets text*)

As You Like It, what an interesting title. Clearly there's a hidden message here. A hidden message from Mr. Shakespeare himself. It's not *As You Like It*, it's "As **YOU** Like It." A romantic comedy with a happy ending; four couples, none gay, all, by the end, happily married. Exactly as YOU like it. This play is what YOU like. But let's not be too quick to flee the latently homosexual aspect of Elizabethan theatre. Yes, all the couples are heterosexual, but, as you've already learned, all women in Shakespeare's time were played by boys, hence suggesting homosexuality without espousing it, again as **YOU** like it. But I am not suggesting Shakespeare is homosexual. Or heterosexual. Or even asexual. Shakespeare is omnisexual. Shakespeare teaches us through *As You Like It* that all sexual definitions are arbitrary. Gender is a role. We are all actors. In our play, Rosalind is acted by a boy, pretending to be a girl, who goes into the forest disguised as a boy, meets Orlando and, as a boy, pretends to be a girl to teach Orlando about love. Or a boy playing a girl playing a boy playing a girl. Or boy-girl, boy-girl. Am I making good sense? Enough said. Question. Is *As You Like It* a classical or a Shakespearean comedy?

(*waits for an answer*)

It's by Shakespeare, what do you think? It's a Shakespearean comedy. Classical comedies from ancient Greece ask us to laugh with scorn or contempt at the character or characters before us. We feel superior to them. And we laugh and learn from their stupidity. A Shakespearean comedy, on the other hand, inspires us. We admire Shakespearean characters. Why? Because they are intelligent. They are heroically struggling against forces beyond their control. We don't laugh at them. We laugh with them. And in homage to Shakespeare, and to demonstrate your silly rumor has now been completely dispersed, I'd like you to laugh with me now. Laugh, please. Laugh. Yes. Yes.

(*laughs*)

We're laughing. You see, when we laugh, we make Shakespeare proud. And Shakespeare was very proud of *As You Like It*. He filled the play with sayings, "All the world's a stage," of course, but also "forever and a day," "too much of a good thing," "the fool doth think he is wise, but a wise man knows himself to be a fool," and my personal favorite, "if thou remember'st not the slightest folly that ever love did make thee run into, thou hast not loved." So true. Shakespeare also put more songs in *As You Like It* than any of his other plays. Countless luminous characters; Rosalind and . . . no, well, just Rosalind. *As You Like It* is Shakespeare's ultimate masterpiece, even if I am the only one to have realized it. So it is just a little sad that the real flesh and blood Rosalind is not here.

(*pauses*)

Do you remember my first day? My first time with you? I walked in, expecting a class of uninterested adolescent dolts. Sorry. But that is what I expected.

(*imagines Rosalind in the class*)

And there she was! Rosalind, with her hand raised. Before I could even recite my first sonnet, this girl had a question. Naturally, I figured she wanted to be excused—a drink of water, restroom, charge up her cell. But no. She had a question about Shakespeare. Most students detest Shakespeare. And I'll never forget her question, which I'm still not sure of the answer. "Is Shakespeare right when he asks, 'Who ever loved that loved not at first sight?'" That's what she asked! She'd actually read some Shakespeare. And formulated a question. And what a question! My mind raced through a lifetime of failed relationships. How could I answer her? I became tongue-tied. This totally unassuming, conservatively dressed, seemingly unremarkable young girl had stumped the Shakespeare expert. I was stumped. "What passion hangs these weights upon my tongue?" I finally replied, "Ah, ah, that quotes from *As You Like It*, why don't we save that question for when we look at that play." That was the best I could come up with. And after class, after that first class, where I deflected her what you have to admit was a highly suggestive question. Where I had no intention of pursuing her. She approached me. Completely unsolicited. After class. Waiting for all of you to first leave. To have me alone, I suspect. It is imperative that every person in this room remember and be ready to declare, that she started it! I didn't pull one of those "Would you please see me after class." Which, if the lecherous teacher rumor had any truth to it, would have been the case. So all of you are my witnesses.

(*pauses*)

You should also know, in case you are asked, that the reason she approached me was to ask for my help with an audition for Shakespeare in the Park. She needed some feedback. Completely innocent. Or so I thought at the time. But looking back, not so. She was grooming me. Oh yes, that's the word. Grooming. Imperceptibly yet progressively crossing boundaries to gain my trust. Yes. All right, on my part I should never have implied that I had some influence with Shakespeare in the Park. Because I knew the director, or I encouraged her to think I knew him. Perhaps she may have thought I could put in a good word. This is just conjecture. Anyway, I have, and have had, no connection to Shakespeare in the Park. I detest that kind of "let's bring culture to the masses." Shakespeare is for the intellectually elite. The semiliterate have television. SO!!! She approached me, and I started coaching her. Daily. And gradually I developed this feeling that all my knowledge—

my, my, my lifelong bathing in Shakespeare—was being passed on. Being of some use. For very the first time I felt I was actually teaching. TEACHING! No, no, I have always taught. But for the first time I felt there was someone listening and learning. My life's work becoming ALIVE, in her! My feelings of admiration and respect naturally became intense. And that's exactly when Rosalind's grooming turned to outright overtures. Oh I know she wouldn't call them that. But that's what they were. Physical overtures, over and over. Inappropriate touching, hugging, bringing up personal matters. A warning bell should have sounded. But I was operating in good faith, and solely for her benefit. Pure. In that sense, exactly like Rosalind and Orlando. Pure. That's all it was. At least on my part. I remained at all times strictly a COUNSELOR to her. I was just there privately with her to encourage, occasionally flatter, that's not a crime.

(*pauses*)

Theatre acting is not a cold science, it's a warm art involving all the senses. As a counselor, I helped her discover her vulnerabilities towards people, and men. Yes, men are people. She had specific needs that no awkward teenage boy was going to. All right, okay, yes, I was more than a counselor. I guess I became her confidant. But I was never superior. We were equals, friends, sharing. So I started giving her lifts home. Only because it was on the way. And we'd talk. Just talk. I valued and trusted her and her me. She related confidences, voluntarily. I then, I . . . started lending her money. Because I thought she needed some, never to make her dependent or to feel obligated. The same for the theatre books. Which she still has, by the way, MY theatre books, which I do need back. And good luck getting them now! It's important to understand that there was nothing inappropriate. It is what friends do. And that includes offering her the use of my studio apartment—my ex got the house—as a place to study and rehearse. It's very quiet there. No disturbances. So some of these strictly altruistic things may be misconstrued. I only mention them in case if they come to light you'll know they were pure and they were innocent. And in no way constitute harassment. And, I must stress, absolutely never ever an off-color, salacious, prurient remark on my part. Like some teachers I've heard of. "Isn't that a tight-fitting sweater. Isn't that a snug pair of jeans." Professorial perverts, that's what they are. Not me!!!!! And even if the occasional remark from me was borderline, there is something called a midlife crisis, it is not easy watching one's youth slip away.

(*pauses*)

Let me explain something to you, and this in no way applies to me. Teaching school, high school, and college, is one of the few occupations where adult males are exposed for extended periods of time to large groups of very young, very ripe women, girls, babes at the height of their sexual desirability. These adult males have been rejected, dumped, ridiculed, and occasionally exploited, by women all their lives, now they're here! In high school, and the tables are finally turned! And they're supposed to ignore this????? Because a girl looks 18, implies she's 17, is 16—all right, 15. Where exactly are these men supposed to find the resolve? Why not make it against the law for starving men to want food? Obviously these men have a need to remake their pasts. Such a situation would excuse all but the most aggressive of advances on their part. And I am never aggressive. Now look, most adult males have never had . . . many adult males . . . some . . . I . . . have never had a satisfying relationship with a woman of the opposite sex.

(*pauses*)

My bond with Rosalind was the closest I've come. And that's because regardless of her age, she's an old soul. And even though that should be all that counts, it's "not the fashion of these times." And so here we are finally looking at *As You Like It* and Shakespeare's Rosalind and love at first sight. And the real Rosalind, this class's Rosalind, MY Rosalind is not here!

(*pauses*)

Over the last several days, I have been experiencing discomfort. My divorce was easy by comparison. My wife and I spent years drifting apart and we should have never married in the first place. But Rosalind. Sweet Rosalind.

(*puts his hand on his stomach*)

I've developed stomach pains. I think I'm rotting. Inside. I think about her. When I'm alone, which is always, I cry. Often uncontrollably. Weeping huge tears of self-pity. "So holy and so perfect is my love!" She could have given me a reason. Instead of just incessantly repeating, "I'm only 15." Juliet was 14! And *Romeo and Juliet* is the greatest love story ever told. Excuse me, what does that tell you? I can't choose her age any more than I can choose mine. But I can choose whether to be open, exposed, capable of being emotionally wounded, vulnerable. And that is what I chose. And now, thanks to my vulnerability, I might, possibly, and let's remember this is wild speculation on my part. But Rosalind's not here today. And the last time I spoke to her outside class, which was yesterday, when I finally cornered her, coming out of the girl's restroom. She intimated that if she were not in class today, which she clearly isn't, she's gone to her parents, then with them on to the police. So there may be an interruption!

> (*pauses*)

Our university level—although this is only high school—investigation of *As You Like It*. Stopped cold. By Miss Green. And I hope you realize, if this is what's happening, she is hurting you. Oh yes. I'm a Shakespearean expert. I should be teaching at Harvard or Oxford or performing for the Royal Shakespeare Company.

> (*raises his hands as a performer, but then, remembering what he'd said about watching his hands, lowers them in embarrassment*)

Instead life has conspired to make me a high school substitute. The lowliest position on earth. Let me ask you this, what is Rosalind doing today, next week, next month, next year that is so much better than a platonic friendship with me? There may be other men that have as much knowledge, awareness, consciousness, caring and self-understanding as I do. But I doubt they're teaching high school. Rosalind. Sweet, sweet Rosalind. What an extraordinary coincidence it is that your classmate should have that name. What were the chances of a bitter and defeated Shakespeare professor descending to teach high school and falling for a Rosalind, the heroine of *As You Like It*, on your class schedule, today? If this were a play it would be unbelievable!

> (*pauses*)

Of course her boorish, uncultured, Philistine parents, oh, they liked the name. Didn't know Shakespeare's play. There was no thought in pleasing me when she was christened.

> (*pauses*)

One night I got her to sneak out of the house to meet me, and we talked until 6 AM. Just talked. Because I resisted. Said "no." Firmly. Not that there weren't sparks. There were sparks. Eye contact. Our eyes locking. She held my gaze! Held it!!! And from that night, for an incredibly short, incredibly beautiful period of time, Rosalind and I "were all made of sighs." Not that we could go anywhere. Restaurant. Movie. Concert.

Shakespeare lecture. No. No way. Only my car, and my pathetic studio apartment. As if there were some reason to hide. I just need to tell my side. I can't talk to adults. You know adults. They'll make up their minds before they've heard the facts. It's always guilty until proven innocent with adults! And the cops? They'll side with her. Like she's some ripe vestal virgin. And I'm the one who loved. Loved her. Love her. Oh students, students, my pretty little students, "if thou didst know how many fathoms deep is my love." And what was I to her? An experiment? An infatuation? A momentary?— Okay, you know what? Put me in jail! I'll go, willingly. To die. Because I prefer dying in jail to finding out what's lower than a high school substitute. I'll die of a broken heart. You know what Shakespeare says about a broken heart in *As You Like It*? "The poor old world is almost six thousand years old and in all this time, there was not any man died from love . . . Men have died from time to time and worms have eaten them, but not for love." So, I'll be the first!

    (pauses)

It was eleven days ago today, she stopped seeing me. Wouldn't come over. Wouldn't accept lifts. Started avoiding me outside class. She stopped answering her cell. That fucking caller ID! Then I caught her red-handed, taking a new route home, disguised as a BOY! Like that was going to work!—Let's keep some perspective here. In ancient Greek and Roman times a relationship between a teacher and student was normal. Completely normal. There was no concept of inappropriate, coercive exploitation. Intense personal contact with one's teacher was an important part, a necessary part of, of, of a working, learning relationship. And the ancient Greeks and Romans were the greatest civilizations. Oh, I suppose the fact that these were gay relationships disqualifies them. That thinking is homophobic! And, what about Socrates? Hmm? What about him? Socrates, the greatest mind of all time, after Shakespeare. And the greatest teacher of all time, assuming Shakespeare didn't teach. Although some people thing Shakespeare did teach. Socrates, *the* Socrates, freely admitted to erotic excitement towards his young students. Just like me.

    (quickly explains)

I said "erotic," not "sexual," "erotic"! There's a difference. A key difference. Now follow me here. Because who knows the prying police may even question you on this. Sex, sexual desire is meaningless lust, devoid of love, it's beastly brutish, animal behavior. But erotic love is an open, trusting, vulnerable, a desire for perfect union. At least that's my definition. And let's keep in mind some teachers have married students and lived happily ever after. Socrates fell in love with a boy prostitute in a brothel. And his love was so complete, his desire for union so total, that he bought the child and made him his friend and student and lover. That is true erotic love. And now I'm to be condemned for following in the footsteps of Socrates???!!!! Whoa, whoa, whoa! I know what you are about to say. I'll say it for you. A teacher with a student is predatory. An abuse of power and authority. Authority? I'm a substitute teacher, the bottom of the bottom. What authority? Substitute teachers have no authority. When I was your age and a student in high school, and we had a substitute, it was a day off. We devoured substitutes. Ate them alive. Sent them running from the classroom. "Sink the Sub!" We students were the authority! And substitutes were "like flies to wanton boys." We had this song. From French class. We all learned it. A song about plucking the feathers off a bird, only to us the bird wasn't a bird, it was the teacher, and the plucking wasn't just plucking, it was figuratively decapitating, dismembering and destroying. We'd sing it. All of us, to drive whoever was teaching us nuts. First under out breaths. Just a whisper. Like this.

(*ducks down a bit behind his desk and sings very softly*)

"Alouette, gentille Alouette."

The substitute could hear something, but no idea what. Then slightly louder. Slightly faster.

"Alouette, gentille Alouette.
Alouette je te plumerai."

Plumerai is the future of the verb "pluck" in French. We're going to pluck this substitute to death! Singing louder. The substitute is hearing it now.

"Alouette, gentille Alouette.
Alouette, gentille Alouette.
Alouette je te plumerai."

The teacher looks around. Everyone stops singing, and acts innocent. And when the teacher turns away, once again even louder.

"Alouette, gentille Alouette.
Alouette, gentille Alouette.
Alouette je te plumerai."

Then there is no stopping us. Louder and louder finally to a crescendo, and we don't care what the teacher sees!

"Je te plumerai la tete
Je te plumerai la tete
Alouette, Alouette
O-o-o-o-oh
ALOUETTE, GENTILLE ALOUETTE! ALOUETTE, GENTILLE ALOUETTE! ALOUETTE, GENTILLE ALOUETTE!"

An absolute explosion of sound, driving the substitute right out of the class, into the hall, out of the school, if we could do it. Totally terrorized.

(laughs insanely for several seconds, but then suddenly stops)

Substitutes have no authority! So, so much for that legal entanglement. Okay, okay, yes, you have a point, I am quite a distance above your everyday substitute. I am a Shakespeare expert, so, in my case, a little hero worship is understandable. And there's my maturity, sense of humor, charisma. And I taught at the university. Received glowing student evaluations. Stellar! An avalanche of them. I was revered. I can show you.

(takes out his wallet and produces a folded sheet of paper)
Look! Look!

(unfolds the paper and waves it triumphantly, then reads)
"Dr. Keir is passionate about his subject. He's my favorite professor." Favorite! Everyone's favorite! Because I'm passionate!—Not in the desire sense. No! In the Latin sense. I'm sure that's what this student meant. As in *passio. Passio* means suffering. Physical suffering. Like Christ on the cross. I've always suffered for my students. Passionately suffered. That's why the university faculty hated me. My devotion. Jealous green-eyed, vainglorious bastards! They forced me out. Sent me tumbling. Landing here. A base substitute.

(places the sheet of paper on the desk, then continues)
And let's get our terminology straight here. Statutory rape or sexual interference are outdated terms, even Victorian. The correct term, if we are going to discuss this with any kind of maturity, is "I. G. E." . . . "inter-generational encounter." I'll be quite honest here. That never happened. But if it did, if anything unacceptable happened, it was an "I.

70

G. E." between me, an authority-less substitute and her, a very, mature, overly forward teena—YOUNG WOMAN!

(*pauses*)

And please bear in mind, countries that have moved beyond the puritanical accept intergenerational encounters as part of the range of human experience. Holland, for example. Holland is omnisexual, just like Shakespeare teaches us to be. The cold hard fact is this country treats you as children, whereas Shakespeare and I and the Dutch treat you as adults. And anyway nothing happened. At all. As I said. Ever.

(*pauses*)

Except. Thinking back there was perhaps, one very small incident. Nothing more. I'm only saying this in the interest of full disclosure. Nothing sexual! . . . but . . . it may have been possibly me who started the touching between us, inadvertently. You see I was coaching her, for her audition. I am not saying I groped her, copped a feel, nothing like that! I am not an opportunist. But her voice was a bit thin for the audition, sounded artificial, so on one occasion, I got behind her. Physically. To demonstrate. I am a teacher, I was helping her, with her breathing, diaphragmatic breathing. You cannot recite Shakespeare without diaphragmatic breathing. So I—well, it sounds worse than it was, clearly—but I was explaining you have to build your voice from the bottom up. Support comes from the diaphragm, not the—well, I may have touched her breasts.

(*pauses*)

Just a slight brushing.

(*pauses*)

No more than a few times, if that. To demonstrate proper breathing. Normally not a problem, but this was after class, behind closed doors . . . in here, actually. "A great reckoning in a little room." Perhaps suggesting, possibly, from her point of view, however inaccurate, she may have felt compelled to accept my, I won't call them advances, but I did and do control her grade, admittedly, this term—not that I ever threatened punishment or promised rewards, again, as always, not the slightest hint of—but, thinking back the touching that went on between may have been me touching her. Perhaps there never were any overtures on her part. These things are always so unclear. Not that, that, that, that, changes anything. That, that, that's not even, even, relevant! Because we're clearly forgetting something. We're clearly forgetting someone. Someone rather important to this conversation. Sigmund Freud!!! The second greatest psychologist of all time after Shakespeare. Oh yes, Freud studied Shakespeare in English throughout his life and wrote extensively on the plays. Like with most everything else, there would be no psychology without Shakespeare. Now, are we going to attempt this conversation without Sigmund Freud? I don't think so. Sigmund Freud said, "ALL human actions are shaped by sexual needs." All human actions! So what was I doing but conforming to nature? And Freud also said "children are sexual beings!" I know I'm not telling you any secrets. Facing scientific facts does not make me a lecherous teacher. And I certainly can't be held responsible for my own unconscious motives.

    (*pauses*)

This year I turned fifty years old.

    (*age is flexible depending on actor's age; lines can be adjusted*
    accordingly)

Fifty! That's halfway to a hundred. Which I am not likely to reach. Balding, greying, watching my face sag, my youth slip away. "From hour to hour we ripe and ripe and then from hour to hour we rot and rot." And once you start to rot, there's no turning back. Rosalind gave me reassurance, hope, LIFE!!! With Rosalind, I was no longer, at least in my mind, I was no longer . . . I wasn't going to tell you this. I don't know at your age if you can even understand it. But there's a problem. With your rumor, that you've all been grapevining though your cell phones, iPhones, smart phones, or whatever the digital geniuses have now invented that you absolutely must own to further destroy direct human contact. And the one problem with your lecherous rumor. And this is touching on an intensely personal realm which I absolutely refuse to speak about, but since I may be facing imprisonment: I lost my wife because I am impotent!

    (*pauses*)

I couldn't, I can't perform. Incurably impotent, no drug in the world for it. No matter what the erectile difficulty—spam ads for Viagra, Cialis, or powdered rhinoceros horn that bombard your email account daily tell you—I AM AND REMAIN IMPOTENT!!! Definition of impotence, "it provokes the desire but takes away the performance." So the desire was there, I am admitting that. I freely admit the desire. The erotic desire. And by erotic desire I mean spiritual. You've seen her,

Rosalind's not a scantily dressed video game vixen swarming the halls of this and every high school. She's human. And that's why, with her, I didn't feel impotent, suddenly I was omnipotent! No competition or threat, like the menacing, demanding older women my own age who can never be satisfied! With Rosalind there was no pressure!!! And no ROT. A fresh start. Young again. Orlando again. Me!—I'm sorry. I detest professors who waste class time relating their personal lives. Anyway this is high school, you're not paying for this.

(*pauses*)

The original reason for statutory rape laws were to guard a young girl's virginity. To prevent them from being seduced and thus ruined for marriage. Virginity? There's no longer such a thing! Show of hands, how many girls in this class are still virgins?

(*waves his hand in the air and then looks around*)

C'mon, don't be shy. Hands up, way up, where we can all see them. C'mon, wave them proudly! Not one. And I'm the seducer??!! If there's no female virginity, then there's no statutory rape. A fully consensual sexual encounter is NEVER rape. Statutory rape laws are repressive and misogynistic! All right, I am not saying it was right. But you have to look at it from my side. I was a sitting duck for some intelligent female conversation! And anyway I wasn't Rosalind's first. Far from it!

(*shocked that he has confessed*)

That didn't come out right. No, no, okay, let's have it your way. I was just going to teach class today. Course material, by the book. Wasn't going to mention Rosalind Green. Had no intention of bringing any of this up. But you dragged the story out of me. Well done. What I am about to tell you is just between us. Not a word of it leaves this room or I will flunk all of you if it's the last thing I ever do. So don't tell, okay? I may have been, momentarily, cured of my incurable impotence. But it doesn't count. It doesn't count because I was seduced. That's what it was, might as well accept it. The one thing I always give myself credit for is that I never attempt to justify or rationalize anything. So for a time, like some archetypal Abelard and Heloise teacher-student love story, Rosalind and I "exchanged more kisses than learned propositions and my hands returned more often to her breasts than to our books." Of course, in the end of the story of Abelard and Heloise, Abelard, the teacher, is captured and castrated. So maybe that's not a good example. But whatever happened was love. Love at first sight between equals.

73

Because I am just a substitute. If your regular teacher, Mr. Devere, tried anything with any of you, you know I'd be the first to intervene. But I am just a substitute with a drinking problem, which is a disease, not a choice, who came crawling to the public school board willing to take anything. Even this. Clearly other rules apply. Especially if it's love. And it was love. Because I wrote her poems. Erotic love poems. In iambic pentameter. And signed them. Incriminating? No. Proves my innocence. If I were some lecher, I'd be covering my tracks. So it is a love story. A beautiful love story. As beautiful as, as, like, as *As You Like It*. Between Rosalind and her Orlando. I was Orlando. I am Orlando. I am her Orlando. Because I'm not old. Fifty's not old. Fifty's young-old. Jaques—he's old. And Jaques is cynical, with a black view of life, and says, "All the world's a stage." The world's not a stage. We're not actors. We're not metaphors. We're . . . we're . . . we're like playwrights. We're like Shakespeare. We write our own lives. So I don't have to be Jaques. I'm not, not Jaques. Jaques SUCKS . . . melancholy . . . out of songs. I love songs. And you love songs. So I guess I'm like you. And if I'm like you, doesn't that make me one of you? And if I'm one of you, I have no authority. And that's important because it puts me in the clear. So. So.

> (*sings softly at first, building to a crescendo; as he sings he stands on his chair, singing louder and louder, even insanely*)
> "Alouette, gentille Alouette.
> Alouette, gentille Alouette.
> Alouette je te plumerai.
> Alouette, gentille Alouette.
> Alouette, gentille Alouette.
> Alouette je te plumerai.
> Alouette, gentille Alouette.
> Alouette, gentille Alouette.
> Alouette je te plumerai.
> Je te plumerai la tete
> Je te plumerai la tete
> Allouete, Allouette
> O-o-o-o-oh
> ALOUETTE, GENTILLE ALOUETTE! ALOUETTE, GENTILLE ALOUETTE! ALOUETTE, GENTILLE ALOUETTE!"

(runs out of steam, and his singing dies away; laughs in a very hollow way; holds his stomach in pain, slowly sits in silence, after a moment he picks up the evaluation he placed earlier on the desk, and reads once again)

"Dr. Keir is passionate about his subject. He's my favorite professor."

(pauses)

What I told you about the student evaluations of my teaching at the university . . . what I told before . . . what I told you wasn't completely—well—they weren't stellar. The evaluations. They were negative. Only this one was praiseful. This single, solitary one. It wasn't enough to tip the scales in my favor. Not nearly enough.

(pauses)

And one of my students didn't write it.

(pauses)

I wrote it myself.

(lowers the evaluation and stares at the audience)

What's going to happen to me?

(FADE TO BLACK)

Keir at Shakespeare's Globe, London, UK (2011).

Keir on the Thames, London, UK (2016).

EPILOGUE/AFTERWORD

(The epilogue/afterword can be given at the end of any of the three monologues, or not delivered at all. It is the director's choice. If delivered, the actor takes a bow, and then lifts his finger to his lips. Once the audience is silent, he speaks.)

Many of the Shakespearean plays end with an epilogue. An actor, still very much in character, steps forward once the action has ended, and offers gratitude to those present for watching the play. Thank you for coming. If the play has been a comedy, the character will relate how wonderful life has been since the end of the play: if a tragedy, the character will explain how poor choices and immorality have led to great suffering. But, since what you have just witnessed this evening is neither a comedy nor a tragedy but really a mixture of both, maybe an epilogue won't work. What is probably required here is an afterword. An afterword is not a message from a character in the play, but a message directly from the author. An afterword generally tells the audience how the theatre piece came into existence. For example, I might tell you that the author spent many years studying theatre on his way to his doctorate, and sat through hundreds of hours of bad lectures, and set down the faults he saw made by many of his teachers over that long period of time, putting these faults all into one character. An afterword is also a chance for the author to explain his purpose in writing the work, which in this case was to promote good teaching by staging bad teaching. As if to say, "If you wish to be a good teacher, don't do any of this." An afterword is also a wonderful opportunity to deliver a particularly apropos quotation, like I might say, Socrates once said, "I cannot teach anybody anything, I can only make them think." If I were now to tell you things like that, that would be an afterword. But in all of Shakespeare there isn't a single afterword, so an afterword isn't appropriate either. I think the best thing would be to just let the work speak for itself. Good night.

(FADE TO BLACK)

BIOGRAPHY

Canadian Keir Cutler is an actor, playwright, director and scholar who has been performing his original works across Canada and the US since 1999. He has appeared at various theatre and fringe festivals, including six times at Centaur Theatre's Wildside Festival in his hometown of Montreal. Keir has been called "one hell of a storyteller!" by *Vue Weekly* in Edmonton, "gloriously funny" by the *Orlando Sentinel* and "formidably delightful" by New York's *Off-Off Broadway Review*.

Keir has an MA and PhD in theatre from Wayne State University in Detroit, a playwriting diploma from the National Theatre School of Canada and a BA from McGill University. He is the playwright and performer of nine monologues (four of them directed by TJ Dawe) and the author of many plays, including the two-hander *Teaching Hamlet* which he's acted with Brett Watson, directed by Paul Hopkins. His solo works include the multiple-award-winning *Teaching Shakespeare*, which he has performed steadily since 1999. In 2016, Keir performed in the lecture hall at Shakespeare's Globe in London, England, during the Shakespearean Authorship Trust's annual conference. Keir also works as an actor in television and film. He is married to the beautiful, intelligent and trilingual Evelyne. His website is www.keircutler.com.

Evelyne and Keir at the 2010 Vancouver Fringe Festival.

WORKS BY KEIR CUTLER

1999   *Teaching Shakespeare* (monologue)

2001   *Teaching Detroit* (monologue)

2002   *Is Shakespeare Dead?* (monologue, adapted from Mark Twain's 1909 book)

2003   *Teaching Witchcraft* (monologue, adapted from *Malleus Maleficarum, 1487*)

2004   *Lunatic Van Beethoven* (monologue)

2006   *Teaching As You Like It* (monologue)

2008   *Teaching the Fringe* (monologue)

2010   *Rant Demon* (monologue)

2011   *Teaching Hamlet* (play)

2013   *Shakespeare Authorship Question: A Crackpot's View* (book)

2014   *Shakespeare Crackpot* (monologue)

2015   *2056* (play)

Sir Derek Jacobi, Keir, and Sir Mark Rylance at Shakespeare's Globe
in London, UK, after Keir performed his monologue
Shakespeare Crackpot (2016).

Keir (2016).

Keir in *Teaching Shakespeare* (2004).

www.ingramcontent.com/pod-product-compliance
Lightning Source LLC
Chambersburg PA
CBHW041529090426
42738CB00035B/6